JN096084

英語
大全
シリーズ

ビジネス Eメール 大全

ENGLISH FOR BUSINESS EMAIL
A COMPLETE GUIDE

デイビッド・セイン
著

the japan times 出版

はじめに

Introduction

私が来日した20数年前、私はまだ今ほど忙しくはありませんでした。のんびりと日本のお年寄りや若者たちと会話し、少しずつ日本の文化や日本語に慣れていったのを覚えています。

「10年ひと昔」(Ten years make a big difference.) とよくお年寄りは口にしていました。しかし、今や過去を語るのに10年も必要ありません。時の流れは速く、働く環境も刻一刻と変化しています。

ここ数年、パンデミックをきっかけとして生活環境や人々の価値観がガラリと変わりました。当然働き方、また、ビジネスで使われるツールなども一気に変化しました。そのため、使われなくなったフレーズや、新たに使われるようになったフレーズ（オンラインでの会話など）などがあり、英語にもアップデートする必要があります。

今回は、そんな新たな場面でも対応できるようなフレーズもたくさん取り上げています。

忙しいビジネスパーソンにゼロから英文を作る時間的余裕はなかなかないものです。本書では、ビジネスの多くの場面で必要になる基本的な「書く英語」を紹介していますので、まずは本書のフレーズを「そのまま」使うことから、ビジネス英語の力を磨いていきましょう。

本書はさまざまな状況を想定して場面別」に実践的なメールをご紹介しています。仕事の依頼、打ち合わせの提案、商品に関する問い合わせなど、多くの場面に対応できるようになっています。ビジネスシーンを「社外」と「社内」の 2 つの大きなカテゴリーに分けました。その中で、約 100 もの場面を細かく設定しているので、使いたいフレーズがきっと見つかるでしょう。

また、ビジネスでもよく使われているツール「ショートメール」で使える表現を巻末にまとめました。「会議に遅刻しそうだ！」という切羽詰まった状況から、仕事帰りに同僚を飲みに誘うといったカジュアルなフレーズも紹介しています。コミュニケーションを潤滑にするシンプルフレーズが中心になっていますので、ぜひ現場で立てていただけたらと思います。

本書はどのページからでも読むことができます。 今すぐに必要な Chapter から読みはじめ、他の Chapter についても、必要なときに備えてじっくり時間をかけて楽しんでください。

多くの皆様にとって、本書が一助となりますように。

Give it a try!

デイビッド・セイン + AtoZ

目次

Contents

Part 2 社内のやりとり

※本書は『そのまま使える基本のビジネス英語〈書く〉』や『ビジネス Quick English〈メール〉』の内容を基に大幅に加筆・修正したものです。

・編集協力：廣岡アテナ、シェリー・ヘイスティングス、深津匡、デイビッド・シーザー、マイケル・ダイニンガー
・装丁：竹内雄二
・本文デザイン・DTP 組版：清水裕久（PescoPaint）
・イラスト：小辻結

本書の構成と使い方

❶ Part

本書は、Part 0「英文ビジネスメールの基本」、Part 1「社外とのやりとり」とPart 2「社内のやりとり」、そして、Part 3「ショートメッセージ集」の4つのPartで構成されています。「本書の構成」では主にPart 1とPart 2の構成について説明します。

❷ Chapter

「社内ウェブ会議」や「著作権・商標」「クレーム」「作業のヘルプを頼む」「人事・総務」など全18章で構成されています。メールでよく使う約1,800の例文が収録されています。

❸ 場面

Chapterの下位の項目です。「プロジェクトの提案」や「会議に招待する」「お悔み」「リモートワーク導入のお知らせ」など約100の場面を設定しています。

❹ チャート

1.「面会の打診」→2-a.「面会に応じる」、2-b.「面会を断る」→3.「約束を確認する」→4.「約束を変更する」など、やり取りの流れを図で示しています。

❺ メールサンプル

各場面の具体的な状況をイメージしたメールのやり取りの実例を掲載しています。

❻ 言い換えセンテンス

各場面の具体的な状況を想定して、メールでそのまま使えるセンテンスを箇条書きで紹介しています。

❼ tips

実際に英語でメールを書く際に役立つひと言解説です。

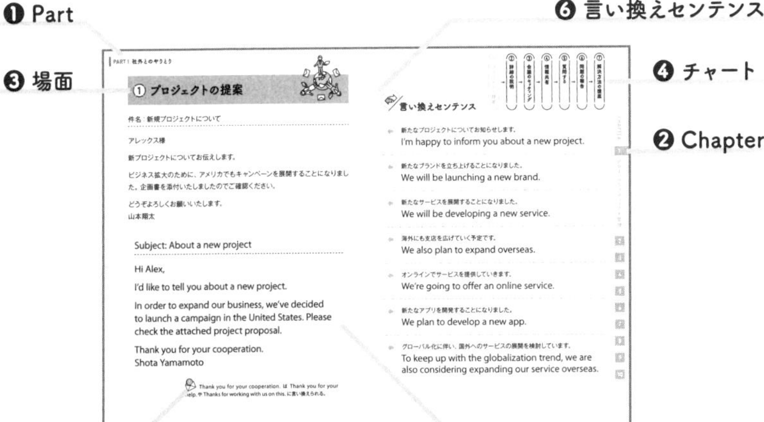

特設サイトについて

購入者特典として特設サイトにアクセスすることができます。以下のURLでIDとパスワードを入力すると、本書に収録している例文の一覧を閲覧することができます。

URL https://bookclub2.japantimes.co.jp/bizmail/

PART 0
英文ビジネスメールの基本

1 メールの基本構成

2 件名 (Subject)

3 頭語 (Salutation)

4 本文 (Body)

5 結語 (Closing)

6 署名 (Signature)

1 メールの基本構成

本章では、相手に気持ちよく読んでもらい、伝えるべきことがスムーズに伝わる、シンプルなメールの書き方を紹介します。まずは英文ビジネスメールの基本的な書き方を学びましょう。

厳密な決まりはありませんが、英文Eメールは次のように、①件名（Subject）、②頭語（Salutation）、③本文（Body）、④結語（Closing）、⑤署名（Signature）の5つから構成されていることが多いです。メールの一例を見ていきましょう。

Subject: Looking for a memory chip supplier ①件名

Hello Linda, ②頭語

My name is Shota Yamamoto from ABC International.

We'd like to ask if you are interested in supplying us with memory chips on a regular basis. (See the attachment for details.)

If you are interested, could you please contact me within the next few days?

③本文

Best regards, ④結語
Shota

Shota Yamamoto
ABC International
yamamoto@abc.co.jp

件名 : メモリーチップの提供元を探しています。

リンダ様

ABC インターナショナルの山本翔太と申します。

メモリーチップを定期的に提供することに興味をお持ちか、お尋ねいたします。(詳細は添付ファイルをご覧ください。)

ご興味がおありでしたら、数日以内にご連絡をいただけますでしょうか?

よろしくお願いします。
翔太

山本翔太
ABC インターナショナル
yamamoto@abc.co.jp

それでは①から⑤のポイントを順に見ていきましょう。

2 件名 (Subject)

■5 ワード以内の簡潔な件名にする

毎日大量に送られてくるメールの中から、必ず相手に読んでもらうために重要なのが件名です。相手にひと目で用件が伝わるように、簡潔で具体的な件名にしましょう。

簡潔といっても、Problem (問題)、Question (質問)、Meeting (打ち合わせ) だけでは内容が分かりません。Problem であれば「何についての問題なのか」、Meeting であれば「いつの打ち合わせなのか」などを明確にしましょう。

また、具体的といっても長過ぎるのも用件がわかりづらいので NG です。まずは 5 ワード以内の件名を心がけるとよいでしょう。よい件名の例をいくつか見てみましょう。

About contract mailed last night

(昨夜メールした契約書について)

※ last night や June 19 のように時間帯や日付を入れると、用件が明確になります。

FYI — Your hotel in Washington

(ご参考までに―ワシントンの滞在ホテルについて)

※ FYI は for your information (ご参考までに) の略です。件名だけではなく本文でも使われます。

Urgent! Thursday meeting canceled

(緊急! 木曜日の打ち合わせは中止)

※ Urgent! だけだと相手が不安になります。このように Urgent! に続けて何が緊急なのかを書くとよいでしょう。

Problem with the new system
（新システムの問題）

Question about the budget meeting
（予算会議についての質問）

Meeting on May 6
（5月6日の打ち合わせ）

Introduction by Mr. Makoto Yamaguchi
（山口マコト氏からのご紹介）
※紹介者を明示することで、受信者は送信者がどんな人物か見当がつきます。

Confirmation email not received
（確認メールが届いていません）
※商品などを発注後に返信がなく、問い合わせる際の件名です。

Top-priority request from Accounting
（経理部より最優先の依頼）
※同じ request のメールでも top-priority をつけることで重要度の高さが一目で分かります。

Defective units in order No. 2245
（注文番号 2245 に欠陥部品あり）
※注文番号を示すことで相手は対応しやすくなります。

本書で紹介している件名やネイティブから送られてきた件名で、使えそうなものをリスト化しておくと役に立つでしょう。そのほか、件名について注意すべきポイントを確認しましょう。

■件名に名前を入れない

日本語のメールの件名でたまに見かけるのが、「山本です」「○○社の山本です」のように自分の名前を使ったものです。分かりやすいのは事実ですが、英語圏では自分の名前を件名に入れる習慣はありません。

■迷惑メールだと誤解される件名は避ける

Thanks. / Hello. / Hi, there. といった具体性に欠ける件名は、迷惑メールだと誤解されて、読んでもらえない可能性があります。また、メールソフトのフィルタリング機能によって、迷惑メールとして処理されてしまうこともあるので使わないようにしましょう。

■動詞を有効に使う

誤解される件名を避けるための手段の１つとして「動詞を有効に使う」という方法があります。動詞を入れることで、ぼやっとした情報を「どうしたいか」が追加されるのでお勧めです。例えば、Need your help on ... (…への協力のお願い) や Please submit ... (…を提出してください) と書けば、受け取った相手は自分が何を求められているのかが分かりやすくなります。

■件名全てを大文字にしない

大文字の件名は相手の注意を引くことができますが、ネイティブは怒りを表すために大文字を使うことがあります。件名全体を大文字にするのは避けたほうが無難です。

■トピックの変更に応じて件名を変える

同じ相手とのやりとりが続く場合でも、トピックが変わったら件名を変えましょう。同じ件名で返信し続けると、あとでメールを探し出すのが大変です。１つのトピックにつき１つの件名を使いましょう。

■件名だけで用件を伝える場合の注意点

ビジネスメールでは、以下のように本文を書かずに件名だけで用件を伝える場合もあります。

REPLY REQUIRED: Attendance at March 21 party
(要返答：3月21日のパーティーの出欠)

ACTION REQUIRED: Please reserve the meeting room
(要対応：会議室を予約してください)

このような場合、本文を書く必要はありません。しかし、空白のままにしておくと、相手が「実は何か書いてあったのでは？」と思うかもしれません。こうした事態を避けるため、本文にNT (No Text〔テキストなし〕) と書いておきましょう。

3 頭語 (Salutation)

頭語は英文メールのうち、Dear Linda Johnson:（リンダ・ジョンソン様）の部分です。日本語の「宛名」にあたります。頭語はメールを送る場面や相手によって使い分ける必要があります。いくつかルールを覚えておきましょう。

■ はじめてのメールやあらたまったメールを送る場合

はじめてメールを送る場合やあらたまったメールを送る場合は、姓名の前に Dear をつけましょう。ここ数年 Mr. や Mrs. や Ms. は使われない傾向にあり、場合によっては使うことで gender neutral ではない（ジェンダーの問題に無神経）と思われる可能性もあるので気をつけましょう。

Dear (Mr.) Robert Brown:
（ロバート・ブラウン様）

Dear (Ms.) Nancy Jones:
（ナンシー・ジョーンズ様）

■ カジュアルな頭語に切り替えるタイミング

日本人はビジネスで相手をファーストネームで呼ぶことに慣れていません。しかし、英語圏では上司でも取引先でも、一度会ったりメールを交わしたりしたあとはファーストネームで呼ぶのが原則です。

Hello Nancy,
（こんにちは、ナンシー）

Hi Robert,
（こんにちは、ロバート）

このように、カジュアルな頭語では相手をファーストネームで呼びます。また、Dear ではなく Hello や Hi を使います。

はじめてのメールで Dear Mr. や Dear Ms. といった頭語のメールを送ったあともやりとりは続きます。どのタイミングでファーストネームに切り替えればいいのでしょうか。

そんなときは、相手の出方を待つといいでしょう。相手が Hello Ichiro, のような頭語を使いはじめたら、こちらも Hello Nancy, / Hi Robert, とファーストネームに切り替えます。

「ビジネスメールにしては、少しくだけ過ぎているかも……」と心配になるかもしれませんが、そんなことはありません。相手がフレンドリーな表現のメールを送ってきたら、こちらもそれに応じてフレンドリーな表現を使うことを心がけましょう。

■ カンマとコロンの使い分け

頭語の最後には、カンマ (,) かコロン (:) をつけます。カジュアルな場合はカンマ、フォーマルな場合はコロンがよく使われます。

● よい例

Dear Robert Brown:
（ロバート・ブラウン様）

Hello Robert,
（こんにちは、ロバート）

● 避けた方が無難な例

Dear Ms. Smith

企業などにはじめて問い合わせるような場合、相手や担当者の名前がわからないこともあるでしょう。そのようなときは To whom it may concern:（ご担当者様、関係各位）のような頭語を使います。なお、Dear Sir or Madam はジェンダーニュートラルではないとされ、避けられています。

いくつかよい例と避けた方が無難な例もあげておきます。

●よい例

Dear Purchase Manager:

Dear Customer Service Account Manager:

●避けた方が無難な例

Dear Sir:

Dear Sir or Madam:

4 本文（Body）

■ シンプルに書く

本文を書く際に意識しなければならないのは、「シンプルに書く」ことです。特にビジネスメールであれば冗長なメールは禁物です。分量は内容によって異なるので一概には言えませんが、長いメールでも3段落から5段落程度におさえるようにしましょう。名文や趣向を凝らした文章を書く必要はありません。簡潔かつ分かりやすく書き、相手の時間を取らせないことが大切です。

■ 左揃えで書き、段落と段落の間は1行空ける

メールは基本的に左揃えで書きます。インデント（字下げ）する必要はありません。トピックが変わり段落が必要な場合は、段落と段落の間を1行空けましょう。

■ 書き出しの決まり文句は必要？

日本のメールでよく見かける「お疲れさまです」「お世話になっております」「先日はありがとうございました」などの書き出しの決まり文句は必ずしも必要ありません。

もし以下のような決まり文句を書いたほうが、本題にスムーズに入りやすいのであれば使うのもよいでしょう。

Thank you for your message.
（ご連絡ありがとうございます。）

Thank you for your reply.
（お返事ありがとうございます。）

I'm sorry for the late reply.
（返信が遅くなりまして申し訳ありません。）

Sorry for the short notice.
（急なことで申し訳ありません。）

Sorry to bother you.
（お手間をかけてすみません。）

■ インラインで返信する場合

インラインとは相手から来たメールの文章を引用し、その直後に回答や自分の意見を書く方法です。

引用する前に、I'll reply inline below.（以下にインラインで返信します）、あるいは Let me reply inline below.（以下にインラインで返信させてください）とひと言断り、インラインで返信することを相手に伝えるとよいでしょう。

► **Unfortunately, we found that 15 of the parts were damaged.** 引用
I'm sorry to hear about the defective parts. We apologize for this inconvenience, and we have taken action to prevent it from happening again. 回答

► 残念ながら、部品の 15 個が破損していたことが分かりました。 引用
欠陥部品のことを伺い大変申し訳ございません。ご不便をお詫び申し上げるとともに、弊社は再発を防止するために措置を講じております。 回答

► **We need the replacement parts by August 19 at the latest.** 引用
The replacements should arrive no later than August 17. 回答

► 弊社としましては、遅くとも 8 月 19 日までに交換の品をお送りいただく必要があります。 引用
交換品は 8 月 17 までに到着予定です。 回答

5 結語 (Closing)

結語とはメールを締めくくる最後の言葉です。日本語のメールで言えば「よろしくお願いします」にあたります。

頭語と同じように、相手との間柄や場面に応じた結語で締めくくりましょう。結語の最後には基本的にカンマ (,) をつけます。

■ フォーマル

Cordially,
Cordially yours,
Yours sincerely,
Sincerely yours,
Sincerely,
Yours truly,
Truly yours,
Respectfully yours,
Yours respectfully,
Best regards,

※ 通常こういった表現は堅苦しいとされ、あまり使われなくなっています。ただし、相手がこういった言葉を使ってきたら、同じように丁寧に返しましょう。

■ セミフォーマル

Warmest regards,
Regards,
Best wishes,

Thanks in advance,
Thank you again,
Thanks once again,
All the best,
Many thanks,
Yours,

※ ビジネスで一番よく使うのがこれらの表現です。

■ カジュアル

Thanks,
（ありがとう）

See you soon!
（では、また）

Take care!
（お元気で）

Talk to you later,
（またのちほど）

Bye for now,
（ではこれで）

Bye,
（では）

Cheers!
（では）

Good luck!
（幸運を祈ります！）

※ 社内の人や何度かやりとりしている相手であれば、カジュアルなものを使うことがほとんどです。相手からもらっていいなと思ったものがあればそれを使ってもいいでしょう。

6 署名 (Signature)

■名前など

結語の次の行には自分の名前を入れます。頭語と同じように、場面に合わせてフルネームで書くか、ファーストネームで書くかを判断します。名前の下に部署名やEメールアドレスを入れてもいいでしょう。

はじめてメールを出す、あるいはまだ知り合って間もない場合は、名前の下に、役職名、部署名、会社名、住所、電話番号、Eメールアドレスなどを必要に応じて記載します。

▸例①

Makoto Yamaguchi
Email: yamaguchi@abc.co.jp

山口マコト
Eメール yamaguchi@abc.co.jp

▸例②

Makoto Yamaguchi
Manager, Public Relations Department
ABC Trading Corporation
ABC Bldg., 1-2-3 Tsukiji, Chuo-ku
Tokyo, Japan 104-0045
Tel: +81-3-2541-0001
Email: yamaguchi@abc.co.jp

山口マコト
広報部 マネージャー
ABC商事

〒 104-0045
東京都中央区築地 1-2-3 ABC ビル
TEL：+81-03-2541-0001
E メール：yamaguchi@abc.co.jp

■ 性別を知らせる

メールを受け取る相手がすでに会ったことがある、あるいは日本の事情に詳しいという場合以外は、日本人の名前から性別が分からないことが十分考えられます。以下のように名前のあとに Mr. や Ms. などを示すことで性別を知らせると相手への配慮になります。

Shota Yamamoto（Mr.）
Mai Suzuki (Ms.)

ただし、ここ数年、性別に関する言葉への扱いがとても慎重になっています。今では性別は「男と女」だけではないという考え方に変わってきているからです。

自己紹介を促す際、今アメリカでは、Please tell us your name, your pronouns and a little about yourself. のような言い方が増えています。

直訳だと、「お名前とあなたの代名詞とあなたについて少し聞かせてください」ですが、つまり He や She などどう呼ばれたいか、どのジェンダーで扱われたいかを尋ねています。

こういった質問に答えるときは、I'm David Thayne, and my preferred pronouns are he and him. などと答えますので覚えておきましょう。

PART 1
社外とのやりとり

CHAPTER 1
グローバルなプロジェクト管理

①プロジェクトの提案 → ②詳細の説明 → ③会議のセッティング → ④情報共有 → ⑤質問する → ⑥問題の報告 → ⑦解決方法の提案

① プロジェクトの提案

件名：新規プロジェクトについて

アレックス様

新プロジェクトについてお伝えします。

ビジネス拡大のために、アメリカでもキャンペーンを展開することになりました。企画書を添付いたしましたのでご確認ください。

どうぞよろしくお願いいたします。
山本翔太

Subject: About a new project

Hi Alex,

I'd like to tell you about a new project.

In order to expand our business, we've decided to launch a campaign in the United States. Please check the attached project proposal.

Thank you for your cooperation.
Shota Yamamoto

Thank you for your cooperation. は Thank you for your help. や Thanks for working with us on this. に言い換えられる。

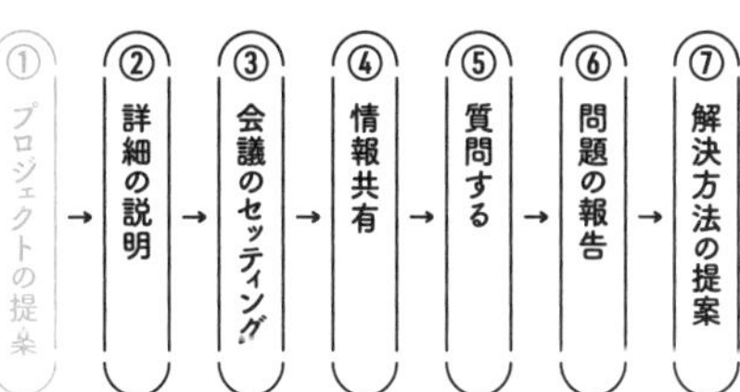

言い換えセンテンス

新たなプロジェクトについてお知らせします。

I'm happy to inform you about a new project.

新たなブランドを立ち上げることになりました。

We will be launching a new brand.

新たなサービスを展開することになりました。

We will be developing a new service.

海外にも支店を広げていく予定です。

We also plan to expand overseas.

オンラインでサービスを提供していきます。

We're going to offer an online service.

新たなアプリを開発することになりました。

We plan to develop a new app.

グローバル化に伴い、国外へのサービスの展開を検討しています。

To keep up with the globalization trend, we are also considering expanding our service overseas.

若者だけではなく、シニア層も取り込むのが目的です。

We plan to target the older demographic in addition to the younger market.

利用者数を増やすためです。

This is in order to increase the number of users.

顧客の幅を広げるためです。

The aim is to expand our customer base.

新しい分野への進出を考えております。

We're thinking about expanding into a new field.

事業の転換を考えています。

We're considering changing industries.

資料をまとめましたので、共有させていただきます。

I've put together some documents that I'd like to share with you.

これらの資料は他社へ公開しないでください。

- Please don't show these documents to anyone.
- Please keep this confidential.
- Please don't share these documents with anyone.
- Please don't show these documents to anyone.

ご協力ありがとうございます。

- I appreciate your cooperation.
- Thank you for your cooperation.
- Thank you for all your help.
- Thanks for working with us on this.

皆様のお力添えがプロジェクト成功の鍵になります。

Your assistance will be the key to success with this project.

② 詳細の説明

件名：新規プロジェクトの計画

エレン様

先日お話した新プロジェクトの詳細が決まりましたのでお知らせいたします。

貴社には新製品のプロモーションをお願いしたいと考えております。

12 月上旬開始が目標です。

翔太

Subject: New project plan

Hi Ellen,

This is to let you know that the details of the new project we discussed the other day have been finalized.

We'd like to ask your company to do the promotion for this new product.

We're aiming to start the campaign in early December.

Shota

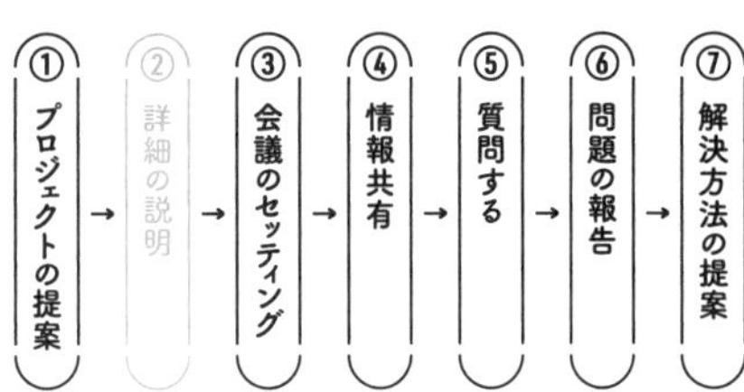

言い換えセンテンス

新製品の PR キャンペーンをお願いします。

We'd like to ask you to do the promotion campaign for the new product.

プロジェクトの詳細は以下の通りです。

Details of the new project are below.

貴社と共同で販促活動をしたいと思います。

We'd like to work with you on the sales promotion.

顧客リストの作成をお願いします。

We'd like to ask you to draw up a list of customers.

> We'd like to ask you to ... は初めて依頼する場合に使う表現。一方、We'd like you to ... は We'd like to ask you to ... に比べると少し上から目線でお願いしているように聞こえる。少し命令口調のニュアンスになる。

イベントの特設サイトを 6 月に立ち上げたいと考えています。

We'd like to launch the special website for the event in June.

製品のデザインを貴社にお願いしたいと考えております。

We'd like to ask you to design the product.

貴社で販促品を作っていただきたいと思います。

We'd like to ask you to create the sales promotion product.

貴社でイベントのプロデュースをしていただきたいと考えております。

We'd like to ask you to produce the event.

貴社と共同開発をしたいと考えております。

We'd like to jointly work on development with you.

貴社のプロモーション活動のお手伝いをしていきたいと考えております。

We'd like to assist you with promotional activities.

貴社の技術をぜひ活用させていただきたいと考えております。

We'd like to utilize your technology.

内容をかためるための打ち合わせをお願いします。

We'd like to have a meeting to confirm the details.

試作品を２カ月ほどで仕上げていただけますでしょうか？

Would it be possible to have the prototype ready in two months?

来年の４月にサービス開始が目標です。

We're aiming to start the service from April next year.

できるだけ早くリリースしたいと考えております。

We want to release it as soon as possible.

お力添えをお願いします。

Thank you for your support.

ご意見があればお聞かせください。

If you have any thoughts, please let me know.

お返事をお待ちしております。

I'm looking forward to your reply.

③ 会議のセッティング

件名：進捗会議のご提案

チームの皆様

本プロジェクトへのお力添え、誠にありがとうございます。

プロジェクトが佳境を迎える前に、進捗を確認する会議をしたいと思います。アジェンダを添付したのでご確認ください。

質問があれば私宛に直接メールをください。

山本翔太

Subject: Meeting proposal

Hello everyone,

Thank you all for your work on this project.

Before we get to the busiest part of the project, I'd like to have a meeting to check on our progress. Please take a look at the attached agenda.

If you have any questions, please email me directly.

Shota Yamamoto

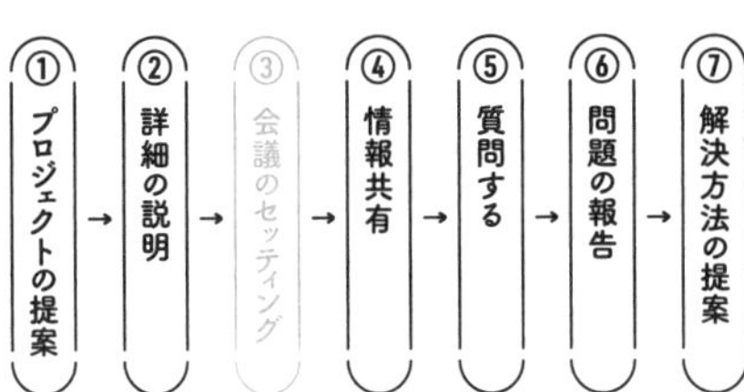

言い換えセンテンス

プロジェクトへのご尽力ありがとうございます。

Thank you for all your hard work on this project.

おかげさまでプロジェクトも順調に進んでいるようです。

Things seem to be going well so far.

進捗状況の確認のため会議を開くことになりました。

I'd like to hold a meeting to check on how things are progressing.

お互いの認識が合っているか確認するために会議を開催します。

We'll hold a meeting to make sure everyone is on the same page.

プロジェクトの進捗状況を報告してください。

Please update me on the progress.

担当パートの進捗状況を発表してください。

Please update me on the progress of area you are responsible for.

必要であれば資料をそれぞれご用意ください。

Please prepare any materials you may need.

プロジェクターなど必要なものがあればお知らせください。

Please let me know if you need a projector or other equipment.

参加メンバーは以下の通りです。

The following people will join the meeting:

メールをお送りしている方々が参加メンバーになります。

Everyone who receives this email will need to participate.

販売部の遠藤と佐々木も参加予定です。

Endo-san and Sasaki-san from the sales department will also be joining us.

弊社からは山本、鈴木、マドックスの 3 名で参加する予定です。

Yamamoto-san, Suzuki-san and Maddox-san from our company will also be joining.

英語圏では自分の会社の人でも last name だけで呼ぶことはまずない。多くの外資系企業では全員に対して -san を使うことが多い。

アジェンダの内容について質問があればご連絡ください。

Please let me know if you have any questions about the agenda.

会議の日程に不都合があればご連絡ください。

If the meeting time doesn't fit your schedule, please let me know.

ほかにも参加すべきメンバーがいればお知らせください。

Please let me know if you think there is anyone else who should join the meeting.

今回のミーティングは弊社の鈴木は参加しません。

Suzuki-san won't be attending this meeting.

漏れているメンバーがいればお知らせください。

Please let me know if I've forgotten anyone.

④ 情報共有

件名：開催地の変更について

皆様

企画会議の結果について、ご報告いたします。

キャンペーンの開催地は２カ所から以下の４カ所へと変更になりました。
新宿、渋谷、横浜、船橋

詳細については、明日またメールします。

よろしくお願いします。
山本翔太

Subject: About some venue changes

Hello everyone,

This is to let you know about the results of the planning meeting.

The campaign locations have changed from two venues to the four venues below:
- Shinjuku
- Shibuya
- Yokohama
- Funabashi

I will email you again tomorrow with more details.

Thank you,
Shota Yamamoto

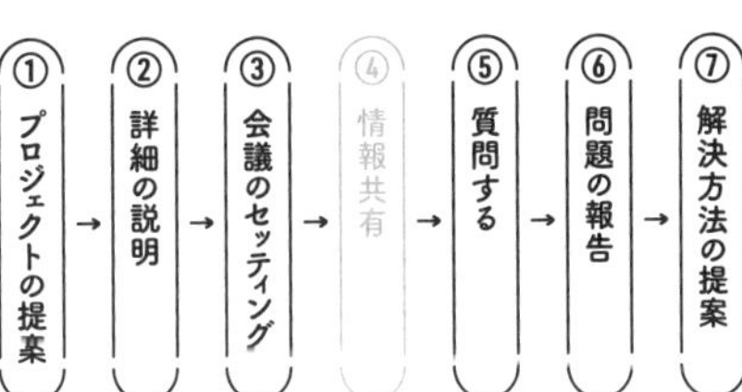

言い換えセンテンス

会議で決まった変更点についてお知らせします。

This is to let you know about some changes we agreed on during the meeting.

会議での変更点をお知らせします。

We will inform you of any changes made during the meeting.

変更点は以下の通りです。

The changes are as follows:

予算額が以下の通り変更となりました。

The budget estimate has changed as shown below.

会議で決めた開催地について共有します。

Here are the venues that we decided on in the meeting.

開催地は以下の通りです。

The venues are as follows:

キャンペーンの時期について以下のように決定しました。

The campaign period has been decided as follows:

料金設定の変更は、以下の通りです。
The changes to the prices are as follows:

料金の設定について話し合いましたが、まだ未確定です。
We discussed changing the prices, but we haven't decided yet.

アメリカでの販売価格は以下の通り決定しました。
The US prices have been decided as below.

会議で変更となったのは以下の３点です。
The three changes that were made during the meeting are as shown below.

変更点について質問があれば連絡をください。
Please let me know if you have any questions about the changes.

私の認識が間違っていたらご指摘ください。
Please let me know if I've misunderstood anything.

変更点について異議があればご連絡ください。
Please let me know if you have any objections to the changes.

こちらの思い違いがあれば教えてください。

Please let me know if there have been any misunderstandings on our part.

この変更を知らせるべき必要のある人がほかにいれば、教えてください。

Please let me know if there are any other people who should know about these changes.

会議で決まったことは以下の通りです。

This is what we decided during the meeting.

認識に相違がある場合はご連絡ください。

Please let us know if there are any discrepancies.

⑤ 質問する

件名：プロジェクトの内容について質問です

翔太様

先日はプロジェクトの内容についてのご説明ありがとうございました。念のため何点か確認させていただきます。

プロジェクトの開始時期は来年ということでよろしいでしょうか？ また、コスト面についてはこれから話し合うということでよろしいですか？

お忙しい中恐縮ですが、お返事をお待ちしております。

よろしくお願いします。
メアリ

Subject: Question regarding project details

Hi Shota,

Thank you for explaining the project the other day. I'd like to confirm a couple of points just in case.

The project will start next year, correct? Also, is it okay if we discuss the costs at a later date?

Sorry to bother you, but I would appreciate a reply.

Thanks,
Mary

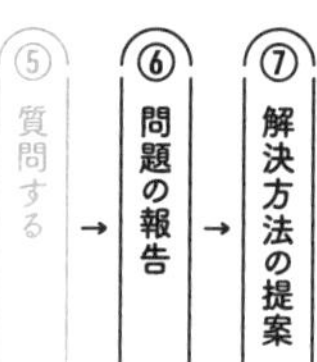

言い換えセンテンス

プロジェクトの内容についてお知らせいただき、ありがとうございます。
Thank you for letting me know about the project details.

新規プロジェクトのお知らせありがとうございます。
Thank you for letting me know about the new project.

プロジェクトの内容について確認させてください。
Let me confirm the project details.

詳しい日程をお送りいただけますか？
Could I ask you to send a more detailed schedule?

お電話で内容を確認させていただいてもよろしいでしょうか？
Could I call you to confirm some details?

作業内容については問題ないと思います。
I don't think there are any problems with the work.

プロジェクトの詳細が分かりました。
I understand the project details.

弊社でお受けできるか確認いたします。
I'll check to see if we can handle it.

作業内容について質問がいくつかあります。
I have some questions about the details.

弊社にとってその日程が現実的か確認します。
I'll check to see if that schedule is practical for us.

試作品はいつまでにご用意すればいいですか？
By when would you like the prototype to be ready?

実際に作業をする者から連絡させます。
I'll have the person who will do the actual work contact you.

以下の 2 点を確認させてください。
I'd like to confirm the following two points:

発売時期について少し変更することはできますか？
Is it possible to change the release date a little?

的確なご指示ありがとうございます。
Thank you for your precise instructions.

いくつか不明点があるので、お電話を差し上げてもよろしいでしょうか？

I have a few things I'd like to confirm, so would it be okay if I called you?

お声がけありがとうございました。

Thank you for contacting us.

あらためて担当者から連絡させていただきます。

I'll have the person in charge contact you.

⑥ 問題の報告

件名：年末キャンペーンの現状報告

スティーブ様

現状の問題点をお伝えいたします。

チーム内でうまく意思の疎通ができていないようです。一度ミーティングを行う必要があると思います。

よろしくお願いします。
山本翔太

Subject: Year-end campaign status update

Hi Steve,

This is to let you know about a current problem.

It seems that the team isn't communicating well, so it might be necessary to have a meeting.

Regards,
Shota Yamamoto

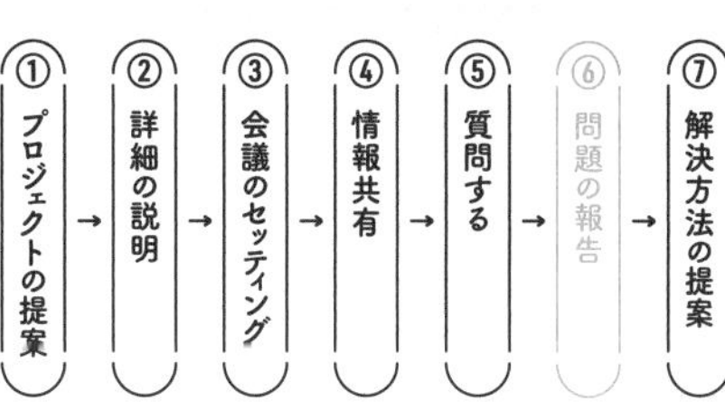

言い換えセンテンス

問題が発生しているのでお知らせします。

This is to let you know about a problem that has arisen.

スタッフから問題があるとの報告を受けました。

A staff member informed me about a problem.

進捗が大幅に遅れています。

Progress on the matter has been delayed significantly.

リーダーがうまく力を発揮できていないのが原因のようです。

It seems that the reason is that the leader isn't performing at his full potential.

製品の品質に問題があるようです。

There seems to be a problem with the product quality.

再度製品テストを行う必要があると思います。

I think it may be necessary to do another product test.

作業のペースが落ちているようです。
The work seems to be moving at a slower pace.

賃上げ要求のストライキが起きています。
A strike concerning wages is taking place.

設備に修理が必要です。
Some equipment needs to be repaired.

開発しているアプリにバグが発生したようです。
The app we're working on seems to have a bug.

すぐに修理に出す必要があります。
It needs to be fixed right away.

スタッフ全員に説明する必要があります。
You will need to explain this to all staff members.

この状況にどう対処すればいいかご指示ください。
Please let me know how you'd like me to handle this situation.

再度全員を集めて会議をした方がよいと思います。
I think you should get everyone together for another meeting.

指揮を執っていただけますか？
Could I ask you to take control of the situation?

この件について至急会議を行わせてください。

I'd like to have an emergency meeting to discuss this.

この件について直接ご相談できればありがたいです。

I think it would be best to discuss this with you in person.

このままだと全体の進行に影響します。

At this rate, it will have an effect on the entire schedule.

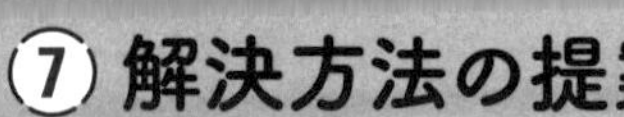

⑦ 解決方法の提案

件名：遅延の解決策のご提案

スティーブ様

チームワークの改善について私の考えた解決法は以下の通りです。

・スタッフはリーダーに毎日進捗状況を報告する
・毎週月曜日にチーム全体の Zoom 会議をする

これでお互いの状況を把握できると思います。ご検討ください。

お願いします。
山本翔太

Subject: proposal for resolving delays

Hi Steve,

Below is the solution I came up with for improving teamwork:

- The staff give a daily progress report to their leaders.
- Teams will have a zoom meeting on Mondays.

This will make it possible for everyone to understand what everyone else is doing. I hope this is helpful.

Regards,
Shota Yamamoto

言い換えセンテンス

カレンと私でこの計画を考えました。

Karen and I came up with this plan.

一つのアイディアとして聞いてください。

Please consider this as one possible idea.

別の部署から人員をこちらへ回してもらうのはいかがでしょうか?

How about bringing in some people from another department?

去年担当していたマイクにチームに入ってもらうのはどうでしょうか?

How about bringing in Mike? He was in charge last year.

外部スタッフを増員するのはよい考えかもしれません。

It might be a good idea to increase the number of external staff.

作業がスムーズになるように新たなアプリを導入するのはいかがでしょうか?

How about introducing a new app to help work go more smoothly?

システムを総点検する必要があると思います。

I think the system needs to be overhauled.

作業をほかの工場に依頼すればいいと思います。
I think we should ask another factory to do the work.

早急に人材育成をする必要があります。
We need to do some staff training immediately.

仕切り直す必要があると思います。
I think we need to start over.

了解いただければ、こちらで対応いたします。
If you agree, we can handle it here.

ご指示をお願いいたします。
Please let me know what you'd like us to do.

この件についてご検討ください。
Please take this into consideration.

早めに決断していただけたらと思います。
It would be good to decide soon.

ほかにも案があれば教えてください。
Please let me know if you have any other ideas.

了解いただけたらすぐに動きます。
We can start as soon as you give us the green light.

the green light は approval や the OK に言い換えられる。

この件は早めの対応が必要かと思います。

I think this needs to be dealt with right away.

この件について上層部と話し合っていただければと思います。

I hope you can discuss this with management.

PART 1
社外とのやりとり

CHAPTER 2
アポイントメント

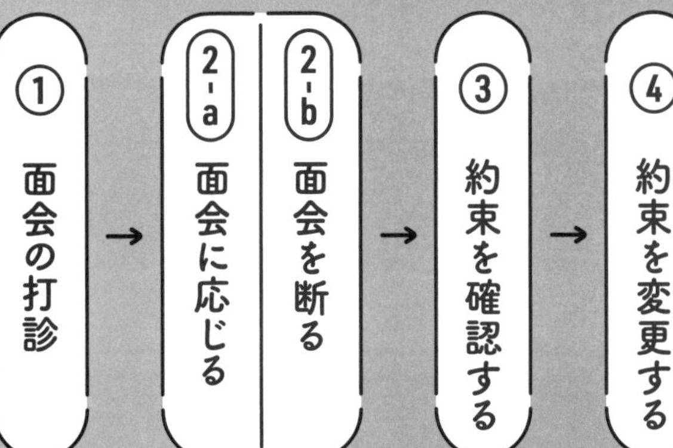

① 面会の打診

件名：面会のお願い

アレックス・ワトソン様

5月27日から6月10日までニューヨークに滞在します。貴社とどのようにお仕事をするかを話し合うためにお会いできればと思います。

もしご都合のよい時間をいただけましたら、必ずそちらのご都合に合わせるようにいたします。

よろしくお願いします。
山本翔太

Subject: Possible meeting

Dear Alex Watson:

I will be in New York from May 27 to June 10, and I was thinking we could meet to discuss possible ways that our companies could work together.

If you could give me convenient times for you, I'm sure I could arrange my schedule around yours.

Sincerely,
Shota Yamamoto

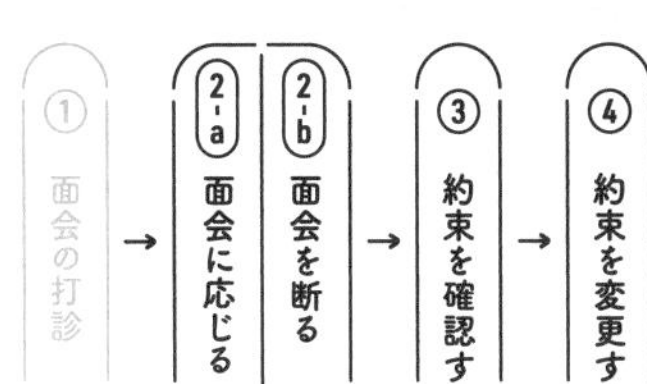

言い換えセンテンス

野田カレンから紹介を受けて、メールをお送りしております。

I'm writing to you on the recommendation of Karen Noda.

インターネット広告で貴社について知りました。

I learned about your company from your online advertisement.

3月3日から3月10日まで、ニューヨークに滞在する予定です。

I'm planning to be in New York from March 3 to March 10.

ニューヨーク滞在中にお会いして話し合うことは可能でしょうか?

Would it be possible to get together and share ideas during my visit to New York?

貴社へ伺うことも、私のホテルの近くでお会いすることもできます。

I could visit your office, or we could meet near my hotel.

今週お会いする時間はありますか?

Do you have time to meet with me this week?

お話ししたい新規のご提案がございます。

We have a new proposal that we'd like to talk to you about.

メールでのやりとりには限界がありますので、ぜひお会いしてお話をさせていただきたいのですが。

Communicating by email has limitations, so I'd like to set up a face-to-face meeting with you.

ご多忙の折とは存じますが、来週あるいは再来週のどこかでお会いできないでしょうか?

I know you're busy, but could we get together next week or the week after?

今週か来週、貴社にて 30 分ほどお時間をいただけませんか? 日程は合わせます。

If you could arrange about 30 minutes at your office anytime this week or next, I'll adjust my schedule around yours.

弊社へお越しいただけますでしょうか?

Would it be possible for you to come to our office?

お会いする際に、新しいメンバーの加藤宏を紹介させてください。

When we meet, I'd like to introduce you to Hiroshi Kato, a new member of our team.

当日お会いしましょう！
See you then!

近々お会いできるのを楽しみにしております。
Looking forward to seeing you soon.

弊社のスタッフもお会いするのを楽しみしております。
Everyone here is also looking forward to meeting you.

訪問日の前日にまたメールいたします。
I will email you again the day before the visit.

近くなったらまたご連絡いたします。
We will contact you again closer to the time.

時間の変更についてはいつでもご連絡ください。
Please feel free to contact us at any point to change the time.

打ち合わせ場所についてのご希望があれば、おっしゃってください。
Please let me know if you have any preferences for location.

2-a 面会に応じる

Re : 6 月 7 日もしくは 8 日の打ち合わせについて

エレン様

5 月末から東京に滞在されると伺い、嬉しく思っております。

今回お会いして、両社がともに協力し合える方法を話し合うことができれば大変ありがたく存じます。6 月 7 日か 8 日が私には理想的です。

どの日の都合がよいかお知らせください。

よろしくお願いいたします。
真衣

Subject: Possible meeting on June 7 or 8

Dear Ellen,

I was happy to hear that you will be staying in Tokyo from the end of May.

I would be very grateful if we could meet and discuss how our two companies could work together. June 7 or 8 would be ideal for me.

Please let me know if either date works for you.

Best regards,
Mai

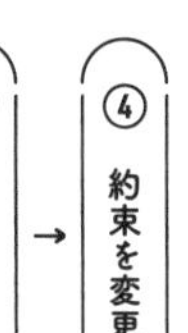

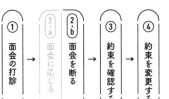

言い換えセンテンス

面会の打診をありがとうございます。
Thank you for offering to meet.

面会のご提案をいただき、誠にありがとうございます。
Thank you very much for offering to meet.

ぜひ面会をお願いいたします。
I would like to have a meeting with you.

ぜひお会いしましょう。
We would very much like to meet you.

当社に興味をお持ちいただき、誠にありがとうございます。
Thank you for your interest in our company.

腰を据えてじっくり意見を出し合えたらと思います。
It would be great to sit down and discuss some ideas with you.

直接お会いし、意見交換できればありがたいです。
I think it would be best if we meet face-to-face and brainstorm some ideas.

お互いのアイディアについてざっくばらんに話し合えればと思います。
It would be great if we could have an honest discussion about our ideas.

貴社のプレゼンは素晴らしいものでしたので、ぜひ打ち合わせをお願いします。
Your presentation was excellent. Let's definitely arrange a meeting.

その可能性を探ることにとても関心があります。
We are very interested in exploring the possibilities.

弊社にお越しいただくことは可能ですか？
Is it possible for you to come to our office?

東京での宿泊先の手配など何かお手伝いが必要であれば、どうぞお知らせください。
If you need help with arranging accommodation in Tokyo or anything else, please don't hesitate to let me know.

いくつかご都合のよい日を挙げていただけますか？
Could you give us some convenient dates and times for you?

私どもの方も、ご連絡をしようと思っていたところです。
Actually, we were just about to contact you.

いいタイミングでご連絡をいただきました。

You got in touch at just the right time.

滞在のお知らせ、ありがとうございました。

Thank you for letting me know about your stay.

ご滞在中、どのような形でもお手伝いできることがありましたら、お知らせください。

If we can assist you during your stay in any way, please let us know.

あなたの訪問を楽しみにしております。

We're looking forward to your visit.

2-b 面会を断る

件名：部品の供給に関する打ち合わせについて

エレン様

打ち合わせをしたいとのメールをありがとうございます。

申し訳ございませんが、弊社では、現在のサプライヤーと長期契約を結んでおります。今回は面談に応じることはできませんが、将来的なプロジェクトでは、貴社との取引も検討するつもりです。

よろしくお願いいたします。
山本翔太

Subject: Parts supply meeting

Dear Ellen,

Thank you for your email and for your offer to have a meeting with us.

I'm sorry to tell you that we already have long-term contracts with our current suppliers. Unfortunately, we are unable to meet with you at this time, but we will consider working with your company on future projects.

Respectfully yours,
Shota Yamamoto

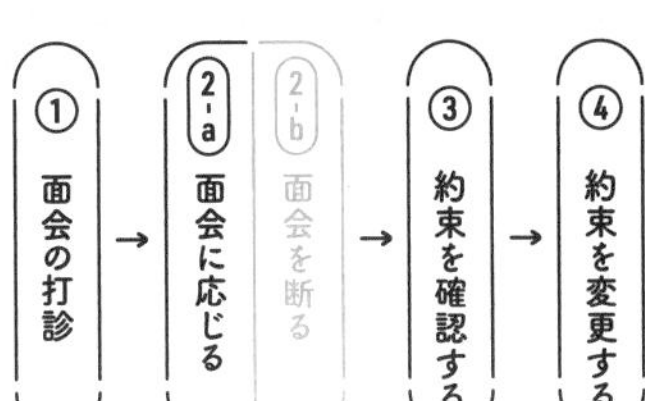

言い換えセンテンス

お会いしたいのですが、その日は終日空いていません。

I really want to meet you, but I don't have any time on that day.

あいにく森はその日出張で不在にしております。

Unfortunately, Mr. Mori is unable to meet you on that day because he'll be out of town on business.

あいにくその日は私は東京を離れております。

Unfortunately, I won't be in Tokyo on that day.

残念ですが、現時点ではこの件について話し合うのは生産的とは思えません。

I'm afraid I don't think it will be productive to discuss this issue at this time.

お問い合わせいただいた件ですが、すでにサプライヤーがいますので、残念ながら興味はありません。

Thank you for your inquiry, but we already have suppliers, so I'm afraid we aren't interested.

メールでお話を進めるのはいかがでしょうか？

Could we start the conversation now via email?

申し訳ありませんが、弊社では現時点で御社の商品の必要性を感じていません。

I'm afraid that we don't have a need for your products at this time.

I'm afraid that we have no need for the products you are offering at this time. はきつい言い方。

ご提案を検討した結果、まずはカタログを拝見したいと思いますので、お送りいただけますと幸いです。

We considered your offer, but at this time we'd just like to see a copy of your catalog, if you could be so kind as to send it to us.

上司とも相談しましたが、面談の前に資料をいただければ幸いです。

I consulted with my boss, but I would like to receive the materials before we meet.

弊社の鈴木が私の代わりに面会可能です。

Ms. Suzuki would be happy to meet with you on my behalf.

近い将来、貴社とお取引ができたらと思います。

We hope that we will be able to work together in the future.

この度はご要望を受け入れることができず申し訳ありませんでした。

I'm sorry we weren't able to accommodate your request this time.

貴社の発展をお祈りしています。

I hope your company continues flourish.

I pray for the development of your company. はビジネスでは不適切と感じる人もいるので避けた方がいいでしょう。

近い将来に別のプロジェクトでご一緒できたらと思います。

I hope we can work together on another project in the near future.

I hope we can work together in another business in the near future. は「違う畑で」「この商売ではなく、別の商売で」。

別部署の者が興味を示すかもしれません。ご興味あれば紹介いたします。

I think another department here might be interested. If you'd like, I can introduce them to you.

当社とのビジネスに興味をお待ちいただきありがとうございました。

Thank you for your interest in doing business with us.

状況が変わりましたら、こちらからご連絡させていただきます。

We will contact you if the situation changes.

ご連絡ありがとうございました。

Thank you for getting in touch with us.

③ 約束を確認する

件名：貴社への訪問について

アレックス様

4 月 10 日に予定している貴社への訪問の詳細について確認させてください。当日は 1 時に貴社へお伺いする予定です。到着したら貴社の受付で待てばよいでしょうか？

お会いするのを楽しみにしております。

よろしくお願いします。
深田まこと

Subject: Regarding my visit to your company

Hello Alex,

I'd like to confirm some details about my planned visit to your company on April 10. I plan to arrive at 1:00. Should I wait in the reception area when I arrive?

I look forward to meeting you.

Best regards,
Makoto Fukada

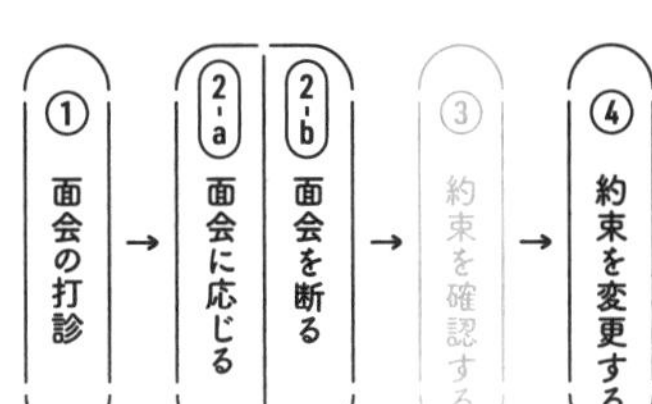

言い換えセンテンス

明日の打ち合わせの確認です。

This is to confirm our meeting tomorrow.

金曜日の訪問について確認させてください。

I'd like to confirm our visit scheduled for Friday.

明日の午後２時のアポイントメントのリマインダーです。

Just a gentle reminder of our appointment tomorrow at 2:00 p.m.

貴社に伺う時間は１時でよろしいでしょうか？

Shall I arrive at your company at 1:00?

到着したら、直接会議室へ向かえばよろしいですか？

Should I go directly to the meeting room once I arrive?

明日は受付でアレックスさんのお名前を伝えればよろしいでしょうか？

Should I ask for Alex at the reception desk tomorrow?

desk なしで、Should I ask for Alex at the reception tomorrow? と言うとパーティーで使う表現になります。

到着したらどなたを訪ねればよろしいでしょうか？

Who should I ask for when I get there?

当日は私と通訳者とで貴社に伺います。

I plan to bring an interpreter along with me when I visit your company.

当日は山本翔太と私がお伺いします。

Shota Yamamoto and I plan to visit you.

貴社の住所は以下の通りで間違いないでしょうか？

Is the following address correct?

当初の予定通りお伺いいたします。

I'll visit you as originally planned.

時間に遅れないように伺います。

I'll try to be on time.

迷った場合はご連絡いたします。

I'll contact you if I get lost.

当日お目にかかれるのを楽しみにしております。

I'm looking forward to seeing you then.

当日は弊社のスタッフも２名同行いたします。

Two staff members from my company will be accompanying me on the visit.

もしご都合が悪くなったらご連絡ください。

Please let me know if you have any trouble.

何か変更があればご連絡ください。

Please contact me if something changes.

では、当日お会いしましょう。

I'll see you then.

④ 約束を変更する

件名：Re：1 月 17 日の訪問の件

アクセル様

申し訳ありませんが、3 時 15 分から部会があります。打ち合わせは 1 月 20 日の 2 時に変更していただけますか？

お手数をおかけいたします。

よろしくお願いします。
翔太

Subject: Re: Regarding the January 17 visit

Hi Axel,

I'm afraid I have a department meeting from 3:15. Could we reschedule the meeting to January 20 at 2:00?

I apologize for the inconvenience.

Best regards,
Shota

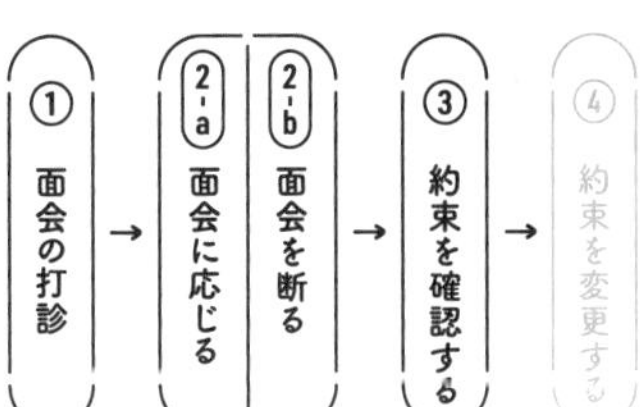

言い換えセンテンス

打ち合わせの時間の変更をお願いできますでしょうか？

Could we possibly change the time of our meeting?

大変申し訳ないのですが森に急用ができてしまい、木曜日にお会いできなくなりました。

I'm terribly sorry, but something has come up and Mr. Mori won't be able to meet with you on Thursday.

あいにくその日は 3 時 15 分から別の打ち合わせが入っております。

I'm afraid I have another meeting from 3:15 on that day.

申し訳ありませんが、その日はお休みをいただいております。

I'm very sorry, but I'm off on that day.

あいにくその日はオフィスにおりません。

I'm sorry, but I won't be in the office on that day.

大変申し訳ございませんが、その日にどうしても札幌へ出張に行かなければならなくなってしまいました。

I'm very sorry, but I need to go to Sapporo on business on that day.

あいにく来週いっぱいは出張です。

I'm afraid I'll be on a business trip all next week.

大変申し訳ございませんが、その日は予定がつまっております。

I'm very sorry, but my schedule is full on that day.

会議の日程を変更していただくことは可能でしょうか？

Is it possible to change the date of our meeting?

Is it possible to change the schedule? は予定全部を変えるイメージ。

会議の時間を午前にしていただけるとありがたいのですが。

I would appreciate it if you could schedule the meeting before 12:00.

ご希望に添えず申し訳ありません。

I'm sorry I couldn't be of more help.

こちらからの希望だったのに、日程を変更してしまって申し訳ありません。

I'm sorry for the change when I was the one who requested that date.

チームが中間目標を達成するまで、この会議は延期できますか？

Could we push this meeting back until the team has reached its interim goal?

他にも候補日があればお知らせ願えますでしょうか？

Can you let me know if there are any other potential dates?

あまりご迷惑にならないといいのですが。

I hope this isn't too much of an inconvenience for you.

再度ご検討いただけると大変助かります。

I would greatly appreciate it if you could reconsider.

せっかく予定を調整していただいていたのに大変申し訳ありません。

I'm verry sorry. I know you already adjusted your schedule for me.

PART 1
社外とのやりとり

CHAPTER 3
あいさつ

ⓐ いろいろなあいさつ
ⓑ 営業メール
ⓒ 久しぶりのあいさつ

ⓐ いろいろなあいさつ

件名：いつもありがとうございます

ヘンリー様

あなたとあなたの愛する人たちが健やかであるように願っております。

今年は大変お世話になりました。

来年、また一緒に仕事をすることを楽しみにしています。

ご多幸をお祈りします。
山本翔太

Subject: Thanks and best wishes

Dear Henry,

I hope this message finds you and your loved ones well.

I'd like to take the time to thank you for all your help this year.

I look forward to working with you again in the new year.

Very best wishes,
Shota Yamamoto

言い換えセンテンス

よいクリスマス休暇を過ごしてくださいね。

- Please have a wonderful Christmas vacation.
- Please enjoy your Christmas vacation.

今年は大変お世話になりました。

Thank you very much for your help this year.

貴社と仕事をすることができ、とても有意義な一年でした。

Being able to do business with your company has made this year very meaningful.

来年もまた一緒に働けることを楽しみにしています。

I look forward to working with you again next year.

昨年は大変お世話になりました。

Thank you for all your help last year.

よい年をお迎えください。

Have a good New Year!

今年の夏は特に暑いのでご自愛ください。

Summer is especially hot this year, so please take care of yourself.

ご結婚おめでとうございます。

Congratulations on your wedding.

お子様のご誕生おめでとうございます。

Congratulations on your new baby.

お子様が生まれたと聞きました！

I heard about your new arrival!

new arrival = 新しく生まれた子ども。

幸せなニュースを聞けて嬉しいです。

I'm glad to hear such happy news.

ささやかなお祝いをお送りします。

I'd like to send you my congratulations.

よろしければ近況をお聞かせください。

Could I ask you to bring me up to speed?

bring someone up to speed は「必要な情報を〈人〉に与える」という意味のイディオム。

来年もどうぞよろしくお願いいたします。

I look forward to working with you next year.

お体に気をつけてください。

Please take care.

末長くお幸せに。

I wish you a lifetime of happiness.

お祝いをお伝えするのが遅くなり、申し訳ございません。

Sorry for the late congratulations.

近いうちにまた集まりましょう。

Let's get together sometime soon.

ⓑ 営業メール

件名：打ち合わせのお願い

ブライアン・フォールズ様

はじめまして。ABC社の小林真衣と申します。

6月に行われた東京でのカーケア用品の展示会で名刺をいただきました。貴社のサービスに興味を持ち、メールをしました。

近日中に対面もしくはオンラインで打ち合わせをさせていただけたらと思います。月曜日はだいたい空いております。

お返事お待ちしております。

よろしくお願いいたします。
小林真衣

Subject: Request for an appointment

Dear Brian Falls,

Appointment request でも OK

It's nice to make your acquaintance. My name is Mai Kobayashi from ABC Corporation.

We exchanged business cards at the Car Care Exhibition in Tokyo in June. I am writing to you because we are interested in your services.

If possible, could we have a meeting in person or online in the near future? I am mostly free on Mondays.

I look forward to hearing from you.

Best regards,
Mai Kobayashi

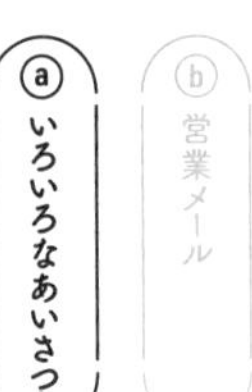

言い換えセンテンス

はじめまして。
It's nice to meet you.

XXX 社主催のパーティーでお会いした山本舞です。
My name is Mai Yamamoto. We met at the party organized by XXX Co.

先日お会いした際は、短いごあいさつをする時間しかありませんでした。
I only had time to introduce myself briefly when we met the other day.

6 月 8 日の展示会でお会いした鈴木から、あなたの名刺をもらいました。
I got your business card from Mr. Suzuki who met you briefly at the exhibition on June 8.

5 月 15 日に弊社の高野と一緒にごあいさつをした者です。
My colleague Takano-san and I introduced ourselves to you on May 15.

ぜひ、貴社とビジネスをしたいと考えております。
I would very much like to do business with your company.

貴社と一緒にお仕事ができればと思いメールしました。

I'm writing to ask about the possibility of our two companies working together on a project.

具体的なことは決まっておりません。

The details have not been decided.

Zoom でブレストなどできたらと思います。

If possible, I'd like to brainstorm with you on Zoom.

手短かに打ち合わせができればと思います。

I'd like to have a quick meeting with you.

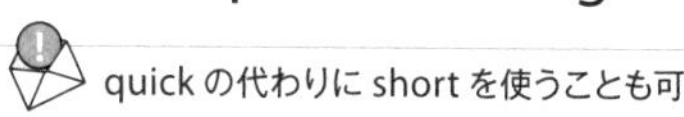
quick の代わりに short を使うことも可。

お会いする機会をいただけたらと思います。

It would be nice if we could meet sometime.

お会いできれば光栄です。

It would be great if we could meet.

弊社の簡単なプロフィールを添付いたしました。

I have attached a brief profile of my company.

このお願いを検討いただければ幸いです。

It would be greatly appreciated if you could consider this request.

前向きなお返事をお待ちしております。

I'm looking forward to your positive reply.

ⓒ 久しぶりのあいさつ

件名：ごあいさつ

ジョシュア様

お元気にされていますでしょうか？

どうされているかと思いメールしました。こちらはみんな元気にしていますが、コロナ禍のため疲れてしまっています。

また、直接お会いして新たなお仕事でご一緒できたら嬉しいです。

よろしくお願いします。
松本尚志

Subject: Greetings

Dear Joshua,

I hope this message finds you well.

I'm just writing to see how you're doing. Everyone is doing well here, but we are all very tired of the pandemic.

I'm looking forward to when we can meet in person again, and hopefully work on a project together.

All the best,
Hisashi Matsumoto

言い換えセンテンス

大変ご無沙汰しております。
It's been a long time.

すぐにご連絡を差し上げず申し訳ありません。
I apologize for not contacting you sooner.

8 月から自宅勤務となり、会社へ行くことも全くなくなりました。
I haven't been to the office at all since I started teleworking in August.

貴社はリモートワークを取り入れていますか？
Does your company do teleworking?

すっかりご無沙汰しておりますが、貴社の皆様はお元気でお過ごしのことと思います。
It has been a very long time. I hope everyone at your company is doing well.

キャリーさんもお元気ですか？
Is Carrie doing well?

当社のスタッフは皆、無事に過ごしております。
Everyone here is doing well.

私は元気にやっております。

I'm doing well.

変わらず忙しく過ごしております。

I'm busy as usual.

コロナの状況が落ち着いた頃にぜひランチでもしましょう。

Let's have lunch together when the COVID-19 situation has calmed down.

お時間があるときに Zoom でもしましょう。

Let's do a Zoom call when you have some time.

そろそろ対面で打ち合わせをしたいと思いますが、いかがでしょうか？

I'd like to have a meeting in person. What do you think?

自宅勤務でしたら、オンラインか電話で打ち合わせをしましょう。

If you're teleworking, let's have a meeting online or by phone.

状況が落ち着いたらランチに一緒に行きましょう。

Let's go out to lunch when the situation improves.

最近お元気かどうか知りたくてメールしました。

I'm writing to ask how you've been lately.

お願いしたい仕事があるので、明日の朝に詳細を送ります。

There's a job I'd like to ask you to do. I'll send you the details tomorrow morning.

貴社の皆様にもよろしくお伝えください。

Please send my regards to everyone at your company.

メアリーさんにもよろしくお伝えください。

Say hi to Mary for me.

またお会いできる日を楽しみにしています。

I'm looking forward to being able to meet with you again.

お元気でお過ごしください。

Take care of your health.

PART 1
社外とのやりとり

CHAPTER 4
会議・ウェブ会議・イベント

1-a 会議に招待する
1-b ウェブ会議に招待する
1-c イベントに招待する
→ ② 出欠の返事
→ ③ 日程変更
→ ④ お礼

1-a 会議に招待する

件名：4月10日の広告キャンペーン会議

ジョージ様

4月10日2時よりB会議室で行われる会議についてお知らせいたします。会議では、春の広告キャンペーンについて話し合う予定です。

もし出席できない場合は、なるべく早くお知らせください。

それでは。
深田マコト

Subject: April 10 meeting regarding the ad campaign

Dear George,

I'd like to let you know about a meeting on April 10 at 2:00 in Room B. We plan to discuss the spring advertisement campaign.

If you can't come, please let me know as soon as possible.

Take care,
Makoto Fukada

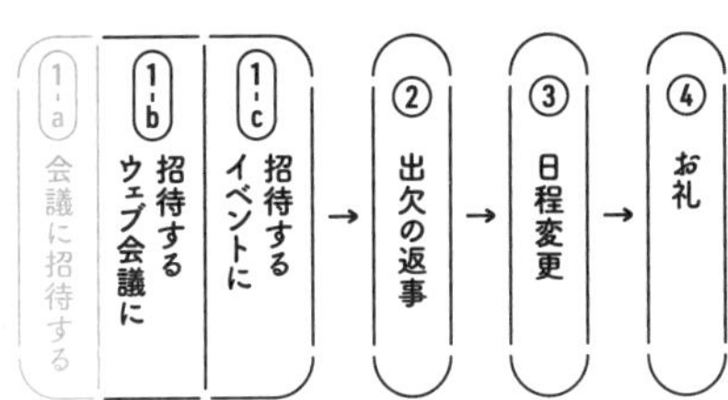

言い換えセンテンス

両社合同の会議を開催することになりました。

Our companies will hold a joint meeting.

下記の日程で会議を行いたいと思います。

I would like to set up a meeting according to the schedule below.

お互いの認識を共有するために会議を開催することになりました。

We will hold a meeting so that we can share our thoughts.

ミーティングは弊社の会議室で実施します。

The meeting will be in our company's meeting room.

当プロジェクトにおける両社の認識を確認し合うのが目的です。

The purpose is to confirm that both companies are on the same page regarding the project.

4月10日開催予定の合同プロジェクト会議についてのお知らせです。

This is a to notify you of a joint project meeting scheduled for April 10.

会議の議題を添付しましたのでご確認ください。

Please look over the attached agenda for the meeting.

会議のトピックは以下の通りです。

The meeting will cover the following topics:

アジェンダは若干変更する可能性があります。

The agenda may change slightly.

キャンペーンの具体的な内容を話し合う予定です。

I plan to discuss the details of the campaign.

議題以外のご質問やご提案も大歓迎です。

Questions and suggestions outside of the agenda are also welcome.

打ち合わせの所要時間は 2 時間を予定しております。

The meeting is expected to take about two hours.

日にち：6 月 3 日
時間：11 時～ 12 時（日本時間）

Date: June 3
Time: 11:00-12:00 (JST)

所要時間：2 時間

Duration: Two hours

会場：弊社 2F 大会議室

Meeting location: Our company's large meeting room on the second floor

ほかの仕事のために出席できない場合は 6 月 19 日 3 時までにお知らせください。

Please inform me by 3:00 on June 19 if you can not attend the meeting due to other work obligations.

大切な会議になりますので、できるだけご出席をお願いいたします。

This is an important meeting, so please attend if at all possible.

1-b ウェブ会議に招待する

件名：Zoom 会議へのご招待

エレン様

11 日に予定されている会議のリンクをお送りします。当日時間になったら、リンクをクリックしてお入りください。Zoom のアプリをインストールしておくことをお勧めします。

当日お会いできるのを楽しみにしております。

よろしくお願いいたします。
鈴木真衣

Subject: Invitation to a Zoom meeting

Dear Ellen,

I am sending the link for the meeting planned on the 11th. Please open the link at the scheduled time. I recommend you install the Zoom app.

I'm looking forward to seeing you then.

Best regards,
Mai Suzuki

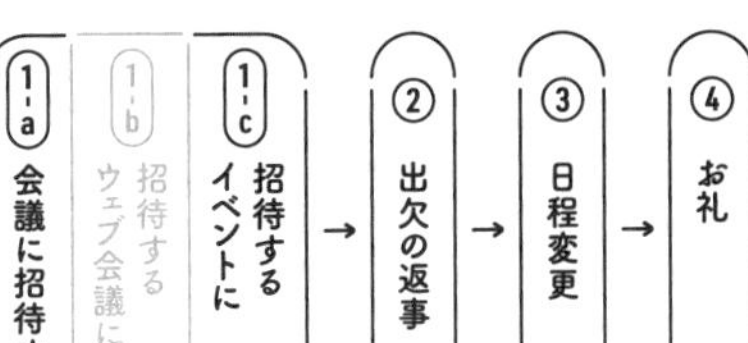

言い換えセンテンス

当日はオンライン会議システム「Zoom ミーティング」を使います。

We will be using the online meeting system "Zoom Meetings" for our meeting that day.

会議の前日に参加URLとパスワードを登録されたメールアドレスに送ります。

I will send the meeting URL and password to your registered email address by the day before the meeting.

時間になったら以下のリンクをクリックしてください。

Please open the link below at the scheduled time.

Zoomの使い方がわからない方はお気軽に私宛に連絡をください。

Don't hesitate to contact me if you're unsure about how to use Zoom.

アプリを入れなくてもオンラインで参加できます。

You can participate online even without downloading the app.

アプリの方がネット接続が安定します。

The connection is more stable on the app.

会議の前日までにパスワードが届かない方はご連絡ください。

Please contact me if you don't receive the password by the day before the meeting.

接続が安定しているか会議の前日までに確認してください。

Please make sure your connection is stable before the meeting.

携帯電話もしくはタブレットからでも参加できます。

You can also join the meeting by phone or tablet.

映像をオンにして会議にご参加ください。

Make sure your camera is on during the meeting.

ネット接続が不安定な場合はお知らせください。

Please contact me if your connection is unstable.

会議は録音させていただきますのでご了承ください。

Please note that the audio of the meeting will be recorded.

録音した内容は会議後にシェアさせていただきます。

I will share the recorded audio after the meeting.

会議の途中でもご質問をお送りいただいてかまいません。

You may send your questions during the meeting as well.

リンクをクリックしても入れないときは、パスワードも入力してください。

If you can't join just by clicking the link, enter the password as well.

会議の開始時間の少し前にURLをクリックしてください。

Please access the URL a few minutes before the meeting is scheduled to start.

ご参加をお待ちしております。

We are looking forward to your participation.

ご都合が合わなければご連絡ください。

If this time does not work for you, please let me know.

1-c イベントに招待する

件名：創立 50 周年イベントへのご招待

アンジー・ミラー様

弊社は今年 12 月 1 日で創立 50 周年を迎えます。この業界の多くの仲間や同僚の皆さんに、一緒に祝っていただきたくご招待いたします。

ディナーパーティーをエンプレスホテルのレストランのフレンチキッチンで行います。11 月 1 日までに出欠のご連絡をお願いいたします。

ご出席いただければ大変光栄に存じます。

よろしくお願いいたします。
山本翔太

Subject: Invitation to our 50th anniversary

Dear Angie Miller,

Our company will celebrate its 50th anniversary on December 1 of this year. We would like to invite our industry associates and colleagues to celebrate with us.

A dinner party will be held at the French Kitchen restaurant in the Empress Hotel. Please let us know by November 1 if you can attend.

We would be honored if you could join us.

All the best,
Shota Yamamoto

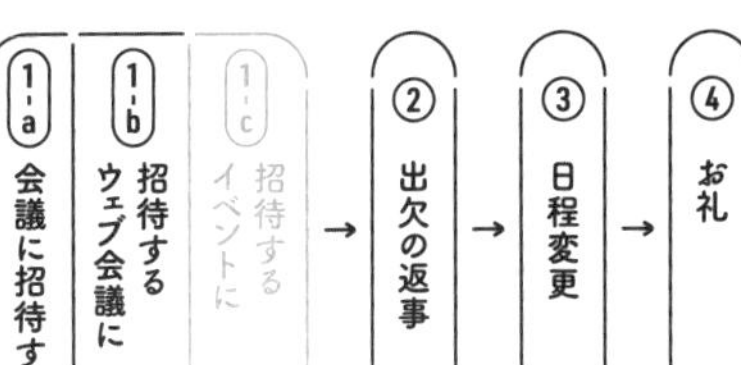

言い換えセンテンス

弊社の創立50周年を祝うために12月17日にパーティーを開催いたします。

We will be having a party on December 17 to celebrate our 50th anniversary.

弊社の新製品お披露目パーティーを開催いたします。

We will hold an unveiling party for our company's new product.

新製品の完成を祝うイベントを行います。

We will hold an event to celebrate the completion of our new product.

パーティーで新しいオフィスのお披露目もします。

We'll also unveil the new office at the party.

弊社の大切なクライアントである皆様と祝えることを楽しみにしております。

We're looking forward to having all of our important clients there to celebrate with us.

製品開発に関わっていただいた皆様へのお礼もしたいと考えています。

We want to also thank everyone involved in the development of our product.

いつもお世話になっているお客様への感謝の気持ちを込めて今回のイベントを開催いたします。

We are holding this event to express our gratitude to all of our valued customers.

イベントの詳細は添付しています。

The details of the event are attached.

ご出席いただけることを心から願っております。

I sincerely hope that you will be able to attend.

お時間が合えばぜひパーティーにいらしてください。

If you are available, please come and join the party.

お忙しい時期と思いますが、ぜひご参加ください。

I know it's a busy time for you, but please join us if you have the chance.

お誘い合わせのうえご参加ください。

Feel free to bring someone with you.

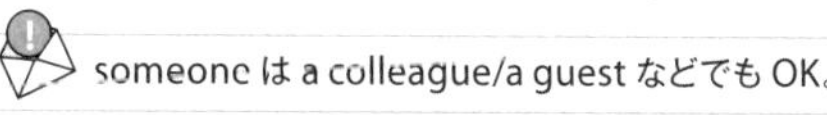
someone は a colleague/a guest などでも OK。

お返事は今週中にいただけると助かります。

We would appreciate it if you could reply this week.

お返事はこのメールにご返信いただけたらと思います。

I would appreciate it if you could reply to this email.

貴社の参加人数をお知らせください。

Please let us know the number of participants from your company.

その日は予定を空けておいていただけると幸いです。

We would be pleased if you would save the date for it.

ご参加を心よりお待ちしております。

We'd be delighted to have you there.

社員一同ご参加をお待ちしております。

Everyone is hoping you can attend.

② 出欠の返事

件名：出欠のお返事

スミス様

ロンドンで行われる会議に出席させていただく予定です。予定ではロンドンに12日に到着します。

皆さんにお会いできることを楽しみにしています。

よろしくお願いいたします。
遠藤真由美

Subject: Reply regarding attendance

Dear Mr. Smith,

I am going to attend the meeting in London. I plan to arrive in London on the 12th.

I look forward to seeing you all soon.

Kind regards,
Mayumi Endo

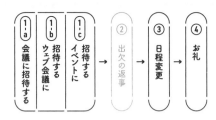

言い換えセンテンス

会議に招待していただきありがとうございます。

Thank you for inviting me to the meeting.

会議に出席します。

I will be attending the meeting.

残念ですが、会議は欠席します。

Unfortunately, I will not be able to attend the meeting.

来月の貴社での会議に出席予定です。

I am planning to attend the meeting at your company next month.

来月鈴木が会議に出席する予定です。

Mr. Suzuki will be attending the meeting next month.

19 日の国際展示会に下記 2 名が出席します。

We are planning to have the following two people attend the international exhibition on the 19th:

ニューヨークで行われる人材育成プログラムへの参加を希望します。

I would like to participate in the HR training program in New York.

詳細が分かり次第メールを送ってください。

Please email me the details once you get them.

帰国の日程を決めたいので、会議のスケジュールを教えてください。

I would like to decide my return date so please let me know the conference schedule.

来月のセミナーへの出席を希望します。

We would like to attend the seminar next month.

必要な持ち物を教えていただけますか？

Could you tell me what I need to bring?

お勧めのホテルを教えてください。

Please let us know what hotel you recommend.

空港からの行き方を教えてください。

Please let me know how to get there from the airport.

空港へ迎えに来ていただくことは可能でしょうか？

Would it be possible for you to pick us up from the airport?

ご了解いただけますと幸いです。
I would greatly appreciate your understanding.

イベントのお知らせありがとうございました。
Thank you for notifying us of the event.

皆様にお会いできるのが楽しみです。
We look forward to seeing you all soon.

5 日にお会いできるのを楽しみにしています。
I look forward to seeing you on the 5th.

③ 日程変更

件名：会議の日程変更のお知らせ

皆様

7月5日（金）に予定していた会議の日程が7月12日（金）に変更になりました。時間の変更はありません。

出席できない方はご連絡をいただけたらと思います。

よろしくお願いします。
鈴木真衣

Subject: Meeting date change

Dear all,

The date for the meeting planned for July 5 Fri has changed to July 12 Fri. The time is unchanged.

Please contact me if you will be unable to attend.

Best regards,
Mai Suzuki

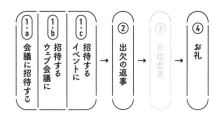

言い換えセンテンス

日にちが 5 日（金）から、3 日（水）へと前倒しになりました。

The date has been moved forward from the 5th (Friday) to the 3rd (Wednesday).

不測の事態により会議は 8 日に変更になりました。

The meeting has been rescheduled to the 8th due to some unforeseen circumstances.

日にちが 1 カ月後の 8 月 5 日に延期になりました。

The date has been postponed to August 5, one month from now.

5 日に予定していましたがキャンセルになりました。

We scheduled it for the 5th, but it has been canceled.

5 日に予定していましたが、都合のつく人が少ないため再度調整中です。

We planned it for the 5th, but we're working to reschedule it since many people are unable to join on that date.

5 日の 10 時半からの予定ですが、時間を少し変更するかもしれません。

We are planning for 10:30 on the 5th, but the time may change slightly.

時間は変更なく10時半～12時までの予定です。

The time is unchanged. We are planning it for 10:30-12:00.

時間が変更になりましたのでご注意ください。

Please be aware that the time has changed.

議題が一部変更となりました。添付資料をご確認ください。

Part of the agenda has changed. Please see the attachments.

社長に予定外の打ち合わせが入ったため、無期延期となりました。

The CEO has to attend an unexpected meeting, so we postponed it indefinitely.

会場が2Fから3Fの会議室に変わりました。

The location has changed from the 2nd floor meeting room to the 3rd floor meeting room.

顧客のホワイト氏の来日がなくなったためキャンセルとなりました。

It has been canceled because our client Mr. White won't be coming to Japan after all.

ご迷惑をかけて申し訳ありませんが、外せない打ち合わせが入ったためキャンセルとさせてください。

I'm sorry for the inconvenience, but I'm afraid I have to cancel because I have another meeting I need to attend.

新たな日程はあらためてご連絡いたします。

I will contact you again regarding the new date.

場所と時間については変更はありません。

The location and time have not changed.

日程を調整していただいたのにキャンセルとなり申し訳ありません。

I'm sorry for canceling despite you adjusting your schedule for us.

お忙しい中すみませんが、日程をご調整いただければ幸いです。

I know you must be busy, but I would appreciate it if you could adjust your schedule for us.

ミーティングの日程変更のため追ってご連絡します。

I will get in touch with you again to reschedule the meeting.

④ お礼

件名：昨日はありがとうございました

ナンシー様

昨夜は、弊社の新社長就任式にお越しいただき誠にありがとうございました。花田はあなたにお会いすることができ、とても光栄でしたと申しておりました。

ご出席いただいたおかげで盛会のうちに式を終えることができました。

ご来訪に心よりお礼を申し上げます。

深田まこと

Subject: Thank you for yesterday

Hi Nancy,

Thank you for coming to the inauguration of our new company president last night. Mr. Hanada told me that he was very honored to see you there.

Thanks to your participation, the event was a huge success.

Thank you so much for joining us.

Makoto Fukada

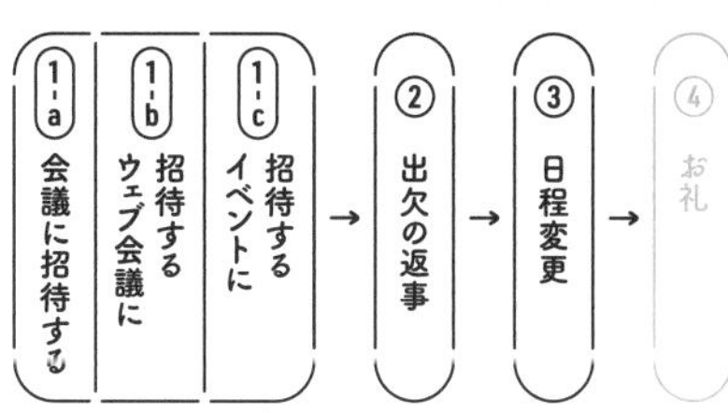

言い換えセンテンス

この度は弊社の創業 10 周年パーティーへのご参加ありがとうございました。

Thank you very much for attending our company's 10th anniversary party.

おかげさまでイベントは大きな成功を収めることができました。

Thanks to you, the event was a great success.

とても有意義なイベントでした。

It was a very meaningful event.

昨夜はお会いできてとても嬉しかったです。

It was great to see you last night.

昨夜はご参加いただき、ありがとうございました。

Thanks for joining us last night.

大変楽しくお話しさせていただきました。

We really enjoyed talking with you.

イベントでお会いできてとても嬉しかったです。

- I was happy to meet you at the event.
- It was wonderful to meet you at the event.

昨夜楽しんでいただけたのでしたら幸いです。
I hope you enjoyed the evening.

お会いできて皆、大変喜んでおりました。
Everyone was very happy to see you there.

参加する時間を作っていただき、ありがとうございました。
Thank you for making time to join us.

参加者の皆様からも好評をいただき、安堵しています。
I'm relieved to hear that the guests enjoyed the party.

今夜はたくさんの方に参加していただき、社員一同感激しております。
We are all extremely grateful to have so many guests with us tonight.

お忙しい中お時間を作っていただきありがとうございました。
Thank you for taking time out of your busy schedules.

遠いところお越しいただき、ありがとうございました。
Thanks for coming all this way to join us.

皆様からの貴重なご意見は今後の参考とさせていただきます。
Your valuable advice will serve us well in the future.

もし至らぬ点などあれば、お聞かせください。

Please let us know if there was anything you weren't happy with.

来年もまた私たちのパーティーにぜひご参加ください。

Please be sure to come to our party next year, too.

今後もお力添えのほどよろしくお願いいたします。

We look forward to your continued support.

PART 1
社外とのやりとり

CHAPTER 5
著作権・商標

ⓐ 使用・転載許可

b-1 伝えるクレームを → b-2 対応するクレームに

ⓐ 使用・転載許可

件名：使用許諾のお願い

ご担当者様

突然のメールで失礼いたします。

あなたのサイトで使われている写真の使用許可をいただきたいと思っています。必要な手続きを教えてください。

よろしくお願いいたします。
深田マコト

Subject: Permission request

To whom it may concern,

I apologize for my sudden message.

I would like to request permission to use the photos on your website. Could you please let me know what the procedure is?

Best regards,
Makoto Fukada

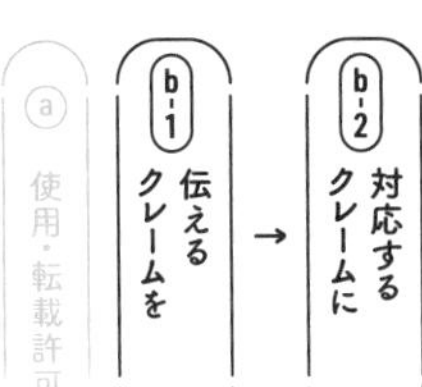

言い換えセンテンス

貴社のサイトに掲載されている記事の使用許可をいただきたいと思います。

I would like to request permission to use the article posted on your company's website.

使用許諾をいただきたく、ご連絡しました。

I'm contacting you about obtaining permission.

いただいたコメントを弊社のウェブサイトで紹介してもよろしいでしょうか？

Would you mind if we published your comment on our website?

あなたのイラストを弊社の無料冊子に３点ほど掲載させていただけますか？

Would you mind if we included around three of your illustrations in our free pamphlet?

貴社のウェブサイトの画像の使用許可をいただけたらと思います。

I'd like to obtain your permission to use the images provided on your website.

使用したい画像を添付しました。

I've attached the images that I would like to use.

使用条件を教えてください。

Please let me know the terms of use.

こちらは著作権フリーなので、ご自由にお使いください。

This is copyright free, so feel free to use it.

商用目的でなければ無料でお使いいただけます。

As long as it is not for commercial purposes, you may use it for free.

弊社のクレジットを入れればご使用いただいて大丈夫です。

You may use it as long as we are credited.

もちろん御社のクレジットは入れさせていただきます。

I will of course include your credit.

画像1点につき、50ドルになります。

The price is $50 per image.

何に使用するのかを教えてください。

Please let me know what you will use it for.

大変申し訳ございませんが、使用は許可できません。

I am terribly sorry, but I cannot give you permission.

使用を許可していただきありがとうございます。

Thank you for giving me permission.

使用許諾のご連絡ありがとうございました。

Thank you for your message regarding permission.

お返事をお待ちしております。

I look forward to hearing from you.

ご協力ありがとうございます。

I appreciate your cooperation.

b-1 クレームを伝える

件名：登録商標の無断利用について

ご担当者様

EFG 社のミシェル・アダムスと申します。

貴社の商品に使用されているロゴマークは弊社が商標登録しているもので、無断利用は著作権侵害に当たります。早急な使用の停止を求めます。

ご連絡をお待ちしております。

EFG 社法務部
ミシェル・アダムス

Subject: Unauthorized use of registered trademark

To whom it may concern:

My name is Michelle Adams, and I'm with EFG Company.

The logo marks used on your products are registered trademarks of our company, and unauthorized use is copyright infringement. We ask that you discontinue use immediately.

We await your response.

Michelle Adams
EFG Legal Department

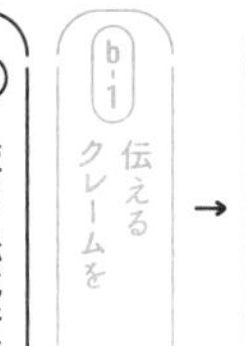

言い換えセンテンス

貴社のYouTubeチャンネルで流れている音楽は弊社に著作権があります。

We own the copyright for the music used on your YouTube channel.

あなたのブログで紹介されている絵本の著作権は著者にあります。

The copyright of the picture book featured on your blog belongs to the original author.

貴社のロゴマークは弊社が先に商標登録したものです。

The logo that your company is using is a registered trademark of ours.

弊社のロゴマークを許可なく使用しないでください。

Please do not use our logo without permission.

弊社のキャラクターの無断使用を禁止しています。

We prohibit the unauthorized use of our characters.

営利目的での使用はお断りしています。

Commercial use is not allowed.

雑誌の誌面をスキャンしてアップロードすることは著作権法に違反しています。

Uploading scans of magazine pages is a violation of copyright law.

使用許可の申請書がございますので記入して提出してください。

Please fill out and submit an application form for authorized use.

著作権者の了解を得ないと掲載することはできません。

This cannot be posted without permission from the author.

すぐにインターネットから削除してください。

Please immediately remove this from the internet.

すぐにこの製品の製造を中止してください。

Please immediately discontinue production of this product.

損害賠償を請求いたします。

We will be charging you for damages.

今後どうするつもりなのかをお知らせください。

Please inform us of what you intend to do.

直接お会いして話し合えたらと思います。

We'd like to speak to you in person.

弊社の弁護士から電話で連絡させます。

We will have our lawyer contact you by phone.

貴社に弁護士がいらっしゃるのなら連絡先を教えてください。

If your company has a lawyer, please inform us of their contact information.

なるべく早めのお返事をお待ちしております。

Please respond as soon as possible.

なるべく早く私宛てにお電話をください。

Please contact me by phone as soon as possible.

b-2 クレームに対応する

件名：Re：登録商標の無断利用について

ミシェル様

弊社のホームページで使用していたロゴマークが著作権を侵害していることが確認されました。すぐに使用を停止いたします。

この度はご迷惑をおかけし、深くお詫び申し上げます。今後は再発防止のため担当者を厳重注意し、さらに著作権等の法令順守を徹底してまいります。

お手をわずらわせて申し訳ございません。

法務担当
渡辺サトル

Subject: Re: unauthorized use of registered trademark

Michelle:

We have confirmed that the logo mark used on our website violates its copyright usage. We will discontinue use immediately.

We sincerely apologize for any inconvenience this may have caused. Going forward, we will issue a strict warning to the person in charge in order to prevent this from happening again. In addition, we will endeavor to adhere to all copyright laws and regulations.

Thank you for your time.

Satoru Watanabe
Legal Affairs

言い換えセンテンス

貴社の著作物を侵害しているのではとのメールを拝受いたしました。

I have received your email about possible copyright infringement of your company's material.

著作物を侵害している可能性があるとのこと、申し訳ありません。

We apologize for the possible copyright infringement.

作品全体ではないので問題はないと思ってしまっていました。

We are not using the work in its entirety, so we believed it would not be a problem.

使用料をお支払いすれば利用可能でしょうか？

Would it be possible to pay for its usage?

使用料の概算を教えていただけますか？

What is the usage fee estimate?

すぐに利用許可申請書を記入して提出いたします。

We will fill out and submit an application for its usage immediately.

直ちに製造を中止します。

We will cease production immediately.

製品を至急回収いたします。

We will recall the item as soon as possible.

貴社の山田さんより、この画像／素材／歌曲の使用許可をいただきました。

Mr. Yamada, who works for your company, gave us permission to use this image/material/song.

使用させていただくことは貴社に連絡してあるはずです。

There should be evidence that we have contacted your company about its usage.

弊社の担当弁護士より貴社の弁護士に直接連絡させます。

We will have our attorney contact yours directly.

もっときちんと理解しているべきでした。

We should have been aware of this.

この度は不快な思いをさせてしまい申し訳ありませんでした。

We sincerely apologize for this uncomfortable situation.

こちらの確認不足で大変失礼いたしました。

We sincerely apologize for failure to confirm.

会社全体でこの情報を共有し、二度とこのような事が起きないように改善してまいります。

We will share this information with our entire company and make improvements so that something like this does not happen again.

何か質問があれば弊社の弁護士に直接連絡を取っていただけたらと思います。

If you have any questions, please feel free to contact our lawyer directly.

弊社の担当弁護士の１人からからすぐに連絡するようにいたします。

We will have one of our lawyers contact you immediately.

副社長が直接お詫びに伺わせていただきます。

Our vice president would like to visit you and apologize in person.

PART 1
社外とのやりとり

CHAPTER 6
問い合わせ・見積もり

- 1-a 問い合わせ①
- 1-b 問い合わせ②

→

- 2-a 回答①
- 2-b 回答②

→ ③ 再度の問い合わせ → ④ 見積もり依頼 → ⑤ 見積もりを送る → ⑥ 価格交渉 →

- 7-a 申し出に応じる
- 7-b 申し出を断る

1-a 問い合わせ①

件名：お伺いしたいこと

アレックス様

早速のご返信ありがとうございます。もう一つ質問があります。価格につきましては、少なくとも今後 12 カ月間は変わらないでしょうか？

本日 3 時までにお返事をいただけましたら、弊社としましても最終決定ができます。

よろしくお願いします。
鈴木真衣

Subject: Request for information

Hi Alex,

Thank you for your quick reply, but I still have one question. Can you verify that the price will stay the same for at least the next 12 months?

If I can get your answer by 3:00 today, we'll be able to make a final decision.

Thanks,
Mai Suzuki

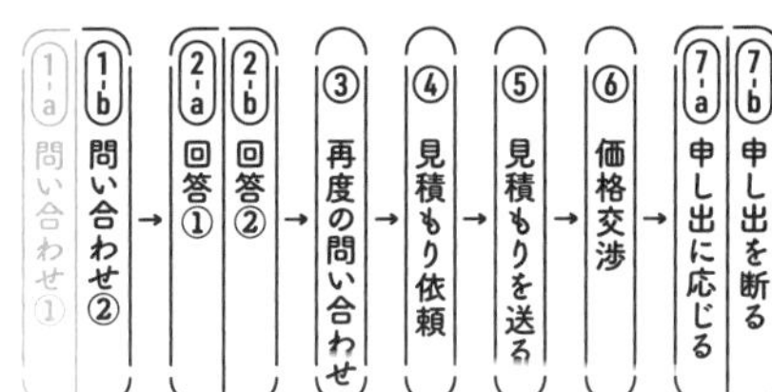

言い換えセンテンス

製品についていくつか質問があります。
I have some questions about the product.

トロント支店のトーマスさんから貴社のサービスを紹介されました。
Mr. Thomas of the Toront Branch introduced your service.

製品について以下のことを教えてください。
Please tell me the following about the product:

最小注文数を教えてください。
Could you let me know the minimum order?

貴社のサイトで見たモデル 525（緑）の在庫があるか教えてください。
Could you let me know about the availability of Model 525 (green) that I saw on your site?

在庫状況については、どなたに問い合わせればよいのでしょうか？
Who should I contact to find out the stock availability?

在庫がない場合、注文に応じていただくまでにどれくらい時間がかかりそうでしょうか？
If the item is out of stock, how long will it take to fill my order?

在庫の確認には、どのくらいの時間がかかりますか？

How long will it take you to check on the inventory?

お尋ねしたいことがもう一つあります。

There's one more thing I need to ask you about.

この製品についてもう少し教えていただきたいと思います。

I'm interested in finding out more about this product.

詳しい情報をお送りいただけたらと思います。

Could you send us some detailed information?

PDF のカタログはありますか？

Do you have a catalog in PDF?

納品日はいつぐらいでしょうか？

Do you know what the approximate delivery date is?

製品の仕様書を送っていただけますか？

Could you please send the product specification documents?

納期の平均所要時間はどれくらいですか？

Could you let me know what the average turnaround time is?

保証の範囲について詳細を教えてください。

I need to know more about what the warrantee does and doesn't cover.

このモデルはいつまで利用できますか？

How long will this model be available for?

今後６カ月以内に在庫の問題が発生する可能性はありますか？

Do you expect any inventory problems in the next six months?

1-b 問い合わせ②

件名：資料請求

アレックス様

貴社のサイトを見てメールしています。

貴社の製品に興味があります。可能であれば紙のカタログをお送りいただけますか？　最新の価格をどこで確認できるかも教えてください。

ありがとうございます。
山本翔太

Subject: Request for a paper catalog

Hello Alex,

I'm writing to you after seeing your site.

We're interested in your products, but we'd like to ask for a paper catalog, if there is one available. Could you also let me know where we can see your latest prices?

Thanks in advance,
Shota Yamamoto

言い換えセンテンス

最新の価格表をいただけますか?

- Would it be possible to receive your latest price list?
- Could you send me your latest price list?

資料請求のお願いでメールしました。

I sent an email to request a catalog.

新製品のカタログをいただけますか?

I'd like to receive a catalog of new products.

最新の製品カタログを以下の住所へ送っていただけますか?

Could you send the catalog to the address below?

貴社の製品一覧をメールで送っていただけますか?

Could you please provide us a list of your products by email?

サンプルを送ってもらうことはできますか?

Would it be possible to receive a sample?

注文を検討していますので、必要な資料をお送りください。

We're thinking about placing an order, so please send the necessary paperwork.

サービスの内容が分かる資料がほしいです。

We'd like some information that explains how your service works.

次のシーズンのカタログはありますか?

Is there a catalog for the upcoming season?

デジタル版のカタログのご用意はありますか?

Do you offer any digital versions of your catalog?

早めに資料が必要です。

I need this material as soon as possible.

いつ頃ご送付いただけますか?

When will you be able to send it?

製品番号 1234 の詳細資料はございますか?

Do you have detailed information for Model 1234?

英語のカタログはありますか?

Do you have an English-language catalog?

FedEx で送ってください。

Please send it by FedEx.

資料と一緒にサンプルもいただけますか？

Could you include a sample with the information?

なるべく早くいただけると大変助かります。

If I could have it as soon as possible, that would be much appreciated.

ありがとうございます。

Thanks in advance.

2-a 回答①

件名：製品の仕様変更について

翔太様

お問い合わせありがとうございます。

お話しした製品（ABCモデル）の性能が大幅に向上しました。改善点を記した説明書を添付しました。

ご不明な点がございましたら、お気軽にお問い合わせください。ご質問にはお電話でも喜んでお答えいたします。

よろしくお願いします。
アレックス

Subject: About the change in specifications

Dear Shota,

Thank you for your inquiry.

The performance of the product I told you about (Model ABC) has been greatly improved. I've attached a description of the improvements.

If you have any questions, please let me know. I'll also be happy to answer your questions by phone.

Thanks,
Alex

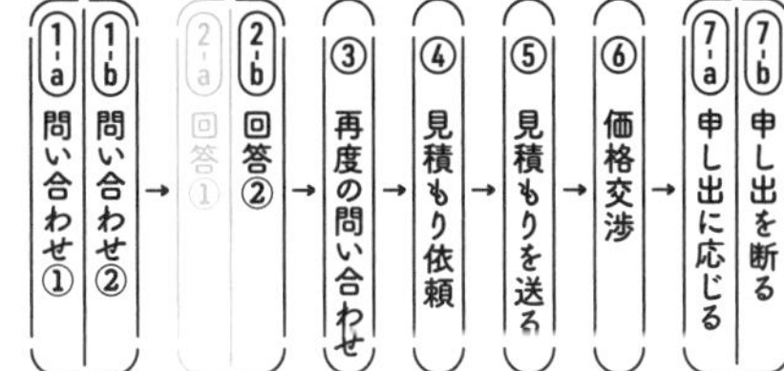

言い換えセンテンス

弊社の商品に興味を持っていただき、ありがとうございます。

- Thank you for your interest in our products.
- We appreciate your interest in our products.

下記が担当部門です。お手数ですが、そちらへご連絡いただけますでしょうか？

The department in charge is shown below. I'm sorry for the trouble, but could you please contact them?

担当に確認させ、早急にご連絡いたします。

I'll have the person in charge look into this and contact you right away.

お返事が遅れて申し訳ありません。

I'm sorry for the delay in responding.

お問い合わせの件ですが、いくつか質問がございます。

I have a few questions about your inquiry.

前回のメールでお話しした件は、その後いかがでしょうか？

I'd like to ask you about the issue I brought up in my previous message.

来月発売する新商品は、貴社のニーズに完全にマッチしています。
I think our new product to be released next month will meet your needs perfectly.

関心を持っていただきありがとうございます。
Thank you for your interest.

お問い合わせいただきありがとうございます。
Thank you for contacting us with your questions.

さらに詳しい情報が必要な場合は、遠慮なくお知らせください。
If you need any further information, please don't hesitate to let me know.

おそらくZoomでの会議も可能です。
Perhaps we could set up a time to talk on Zoom.

よろしければ、直接お伺いして詳細をご説明いたします。
If you would like, I can visit you and explain the details in person.

さらにご不明な点がございましたら、お気軽にお問い合わせください。
If you have any further questions, please don't hesitate to contact me.

この回答が質問へのお答えになっていない場合はお知らせください。
If my response does not fully answer your question, please let me know.

注文の際は、直接私にご連絡ください。

Please feel free to contact me directly if you'd like to place an order.

ご注文はこのリンクをクリックしてください。

Please click this link if you'd like to place an order.

以下の製造元の連絡先に直接連絡することをお勧めします。

I recommend contacting the manufacturer directly using the contact information below.

2-b 回答②

件名：Re：カタログ請求

ロブ・クレイグ様

メールをありがとうございました。

お問い合わせいただいた最新版のカタログと価格表を送付いたします。ご質問やご心配がありましたら下記へご連絡いただけますでしょうか？ 担当の者から連絡をいたします。

どうもありがとうございました。
鈴木真衣
info@xz.company.com

Subject: Re: Request for a catalog

Dear Mr. Rob Craig:

Thank you for writing.

I will send you our latest catalog and price list, as you requested. If you have any questions or concerns, please contact us as below. We'll have a representative get in touch with you.

Thank you very much,
Mai Suzuki
info@xz.company.com

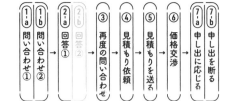

メールをありがとうございました。

Thank you for your email.

お問い合わせありがとうございます。

Thank you for your inquiry.

弊社の製品に関心を持ってくださりありがとうございます。

Thank you for your interest in our products.

カタログをご注文いただきありがとうございました。

Thank you for ordering our catalog.

添付の最新版のカタログと価格表をご確認ください。

Please find attached our latest catalog and price list.

PDF を添付いたしました。

I have attached them in PDF form.

カタログのお勧めの商品に付せんを貼っています。

I put tabs in the catalog showing the products we recommend for you.

ファイルをダウンロードするには、下記のリンクをクリックしてください。
To download the file, click on the link below.

最新カタログはこちらのリンクよりご覧になれます。
Please visit the following link for access to our newest catalog:

あいにくお問い合わせいただいた商品カタログはございません。
Unfortunately, we do not have the product catalog that you are inquiring about.

そちらの商品の販売は終了しております。
We no longer carry that product.

現在新たなカタログを作成中です。
We are currently creating a new catalog.

お忙しい折とは存じますが、ご一読ください。
I know you're busy, but I'd like to ask you to look over this.

ご質問があればお気軽にご連絡ください。
Feel free to ask me if you have any questions.

ご連絡をお待ちしています。
I'm looking forward to hearing from you.

お力になれず申し訳ありません。

We're sorry we couldn't be of more help.

ほかにご要望があればお知らせください。

Please let us know if there's anything else we can help you with.

③ 再度の問い合わせ

件名：ご確認

スティーブ様

情報をお送りいただき、ありがとうございます。

もう一つお尋ねしたいことがあります。234 型の仕様を教えてください。

よろしくお願いいたします。
鈴木太郎

Subject: Confirmation for information

Dear Steve,

Thank you for the information you sent.

I still have one question, though. What are the specs for Model 234?

Thanks in advance,
Taro Suzuki

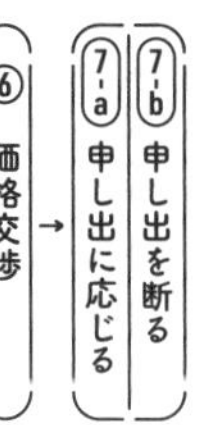

言い換えセンテンス

資料のご送付ありがとうございました。

Thank you for sending the reference material.

貴社のサービスに関する資料を受け取りました。

We received the information about your company's services.

いただいたメールの添付資料を拝見しました。

I've looked over the documents attached to the email you sent.

依頼していたサンプルが届きました。

The sample we requested has arrived.

追加の質問がございます。

We have additional questions.

弊社の鈴木より質問があります。

My colleague, Ms./Mr. Suzuki, has a question.

ほかに教えていただきたいことがありメールいたしました。

I have something else to ask you, so I've sent you an email.

今度は ABC 型と XYZ 型に関する質問です。

This time I have some questions about models ABC and XYZ.

その製品の特徴を教えてください。

Could you tell me about the features of this product?

こちらと同価格帯の製品はほかにありますでしょうか？

Do you have any other products in this same price range?

比較したいので、それらの性能について簡単に説明していただけませんか？

Could you summarize their performance for me so that I can compare them?

この商品の色見本はありますか？

Do you have a color sample of this product?

もう少し詳しく知りたいのでカタログを拝見できますか？

I'd like to see a catalog for more detailed information.

この製品に興味があるので、特徴をもう少し教えていただけますか？

I'm interested in this product, but could you please tell me a little more about its features?

この件について社内で検討いたします。

We would like to consider the matter internally.

迅速なご対応ありがとうございました。

Thank you for your quick response.

今後とも、何卒よろしくお願いいたします。

We look forward to working with you.

ご対応いただきありがとうございます。

I appreciate your help with this.

④ 見積もり依頼

件名：お見積もり依頼

アレックス様

お返事ありがとうございます。

お見積もりをお送りいただけますか？ 5月17日までにいただければ幸いです。

いつもご協力ありがとうございます。

山本翔太

Subject: Request for estimate

Hello Alex,

Thank you for your response.

Could you please send me an estimate? I need to have it by May 17, if possible.

Thanks as always for your cooperation.

Shota Yamamoto

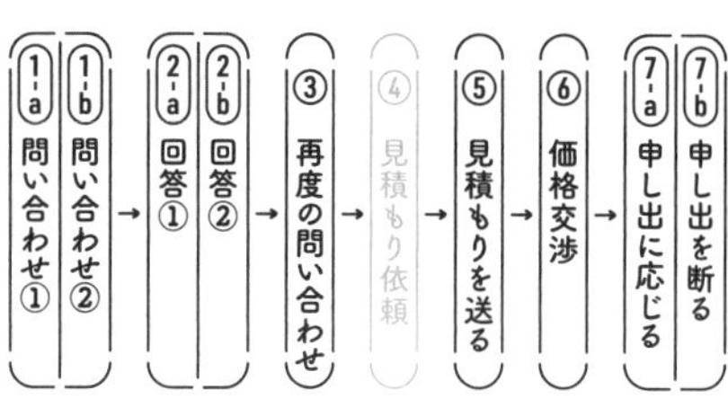

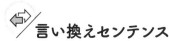

言い換えセンテンス

お見積もりをお願いいたします。

I would like to request an estimate.

以下の製品についてお見積もりをお願いします。

Please give us an estimate for the following products:

まず、お見積もりをいただくことは可能でしょうか？

First of all, I'd like to get an estimate. Will that be possible?

以下のお見積もりをいただけますか？

Could you give us a quotation for the following?

貴社のカーケア用品を購入したいと考えております。

We would like to purchase the car care product from your company.

数量５万でお見積もりをお送りいただけますか？

Could you send us an estimate for 50,000 units?

至急、以下のお見積もりをお願いいたします。

Could you send me a quote for the following as soon as possible?

すでに 500 個の場合の見積もりはいただいておりますが、1,000 個の場合の見積もりもお願いできますか？

We already received an estimate for 500 units, but could you also send us an estimate for 1,000 units?

さらに社内で検討を進めることとなりましたので、お見積もりをいただきたくお願い申し上げます。

We have decided to discuss this further internally, so we would appreciate it if you could give us a quote.

無理を言って申し訳ありませんが、来週早々には見積もりをこちらにいただけると非常に助かります。

I'm sorry to pressure you, but it would be very helpful if we could have the estimate in our hands early next week.

8 月 5 日の会議に間に合うように見積もりが必要です。

I need the estimate in time for a meeting on August 5.

追加費用の全てを見積もりに含めてください。

Please include any additional costs in your quotation.

お返事をお待ちしております。貴社とお取引できることを願っております。

We look forward to hearing your reply and hope we can do business with you.

下記に挙げたオフィス用品の見積もりをお願いいたします。
・デスクL字型 5
・デスクチェア 5（赤 2、黄色 1、緑 1、青 1）

I'd like to ask you to provide us with an estimate for the office furniture listed below:
- 5 ea. desks (L-shape)
- 5 ea. desk chairs (2 red, 1 yellow, 1 green, 1 blue)

今週中にお見積もりをお送りいただけると幸いです。

We would appreciate it very much if you could send us a quotation by the end of this week.

なるべく早くいただければ幸いです。

We'd like to have it as soon as possible.

数社から見積もりを取っています。

We are getting a number of estimates.

⑤ 見積もりを送る

件名：オフィス家具の見積もり

翔太様

ご依頼いただきましたお見積もりを添付いたします。送料を含め、合計で6,100 ドルになります。もし必要であれば、多少の交渉の余地はございます。

よろしくお願いします。
アレックス

Subject: Estimate for office furniture

Dear Shota,

I've enclosed an estimate, as you requested. The total amount with shipping costs comes to $6,100. However, there is a little room for negotiation, if necessary.

Yours truly,
Alex

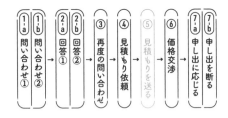

言い換えセンテンス

見積もりのご依頼ありがとうございます。

Thank you for your request for a quotation.

見積書を添付いたしましたのでご確認ください。

I've put together a written estimate. Please refer to the attachment.

弊社のお見積書を PDF で添付いたしました。

We have attached our quotation in PDF form.

納期はいつ頃をご希望でしょうか？

When would you like to deliver the product to you?

総額は 5 万ドルになりますが、これに別途、送料がかかります。

The total cost is $50,000, but this does not include shipping.

価格は税込みです。

This price includes all applicable taxes.

もう少し大口の注文にしていただければ、割引が可能です。

We can give you a discount if you increase your order a little.

以下の通り、謹んでお見積もりをお送りいたします。

We are pleased to offer you the following quotation:

以下の数量割引が適用されます。

We can offer you the following volume discount:

そのモデルは現在製造を見合わせております。

We have suspended production of that model.

ご購入の参考になればと思います。

We hope this will be helpful for your purchase.

ご注文を心よりお待ちしております。

We look forward to your order.

現在流通が大変混んでおりますので、早めのご注文がお勧めです。

At the moment, distribution is quite busy. We recommend that you place your order as soon as possible.

ご注文の際は私宛にメールをお送りください

Please email me when you are ready to place your order.

もしほかにご質問がありましたら、ご連絡ください。

If you have any further questions, do let us know.

お力になれず申し訳ございません。

We're sorry we couldn't be of more help.

またのご利用をお待ちしております。

We look forward to your future patronage.

CHAPTER 1 2 3 4 5 6 問い合わせ・見積もり 7 8 9 10

⑥ 価格交渉

件名：Re：オフィス用品の見積もり

スティーブ様

見積もりをありがとうございました。

社内で話し合った結果、予算の都合上この価格での発注は難しいです。送料を 2,000 ドルに抑えられたら注文が可能です。長年のお付き合いをお願いしたいと思っていますのでご検討いただければ幸いです。

よろしくお願いいたします。
山本翔太

Subject: Re: Estimate for office furniture

Hi Steve,

Thank you for your quote.

After internal discussions, we need to let you know that it is not possible to place an order at this price due to budget constraints. However, if you could reduce the shipping cost to $2,000, we will be able to place an order that will likely lead to a long-term relationship. We hope that you will consider this.

Thank you,
Shota Yamamoto

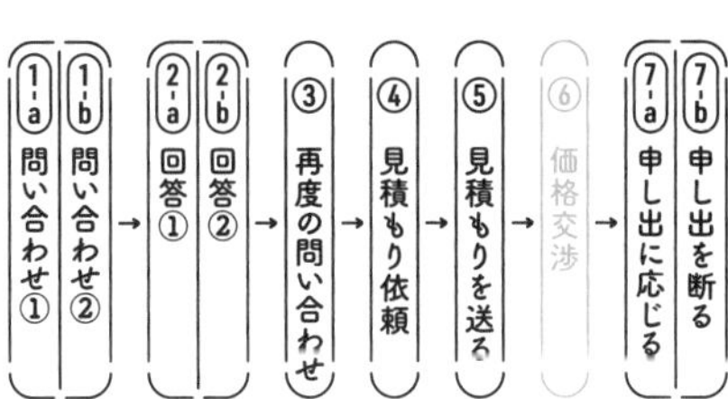

言い換えセンテンス

メールをありがとうございました。

Thank you for your email.

念のために1点確認させてください。

Could I confirm one thing just in case?

見積もりのご送付ありがとうございました。

Thank you for sending us your quotation.

この金額で注文いたしますので、注文書をお送り願えますか？

We'd like to place an order at this price. Could you send us an order form?

お送りいただいた見積もりの金額で特に問題はありません。

There's no problem with the amount of the estimate you sent us.

見積もりの金額を確認後、またこちらからご連絡いたします。

I'll contact you again after we consider the amount of the estimate.

価格をもう少し交渉させていただけませんか？

Is there any room for negotiation with regard to the price?

価格の交渉は可能ですか？
I'd like to know if the price is negotiable.

送料は貴社が提示された金額に含まれていますか？
Is shipping included in the prices you sent us?

金額が想定を上回りましたので、申し訳ないのですが今回は注文を見合わせることにしました。
This price is higher than we expected, so I'm afraid we will not be placing an order this time.

もし送料が含まれないのであれば、少なくとも15%の値引きをお願いしたいのですが。
If shipping isn't included, then we would ask for a discount of at least 15%.

貴社が弊社に提示した価格は、送料と保険料を含んでいますか？
Does the price you gave us include shipping and insurance?

価格は予想を少し上回っています。
The price is a bit higher than we expected.

総額から3% 割引していただくことは可能ですか？
Could we ask you to discount the total price by 3%?

ご協力にあらためて感謝いたします。

Thanks again for your help.

ご検討に感謝いたします。

We thank you for your kind consideration.

弊社の提案をご検討いただけると幸いです。

We ask for your kind consideration regarding our proposal.

前向きなお返事をお待ちしております。

I look forward to receiving a positive response from you.

7-a 申し出に応じる

件名：Re：re：オフィス用品の見積もり

翔太様

この度は先日お送りした見積書へのご連絡ありがとうございます。

再度検討させていただいた結果、送料無料でご提供できることになりました。お役に立てることを願っております。

よろしくお願いします。
スティーブ

Subject: Re: re: Estimate for office furniture

Dear Shota,

Thank you for your email regarding the quotation we sent the other day.

After some reconsideration, we have decided to offer you free shipping. We hope that we may be of service to you.

Many thanks,
Steve

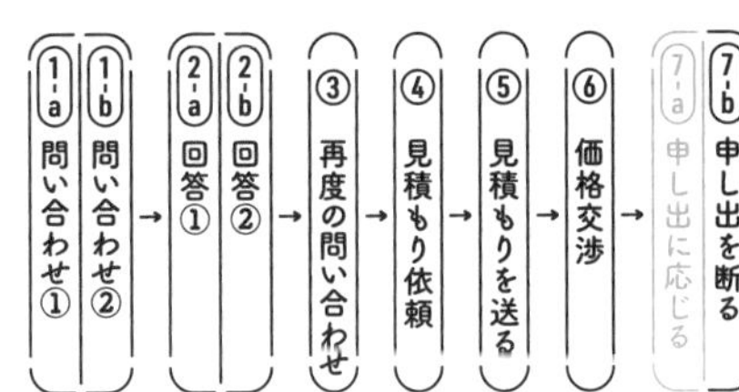

言い換えセンテンス

見積もりへのご返信ありがとうございます。

Thank you very much for your reply regarding our quotation.

値引きのご要望に対応が可能です。

We're able to agree to your request for a discount.

3カ月以内に全額お支払いいただけるのであれば、値引きできます。

We will reduce the price if you pay the full amount within three months.

現金払いであれば値引きが可能です。

If you pay in cash, we can offer you a discount.

出荷日によっては値引きの余地があります。

We can give you a better price depending on the shipping date.

全額前払いしていただければ、値引きが可能です。

We're ready to offer you a discount if you pay 100% in advance.

1 回の注文で 100 個以上ご注文いただけたら、5%割引でご提供できます。

We are glad to inform you that we are able to offer a 5% discount for each order of 100 or more pieces.

今回に限り送料を値引きさせていただきます。

We can offer you a one-time discount on shipping costs.

長年のお付き合いですので、値引きを決定しました。

Taking our long relationship into consideration, we would like to offer you a discount.

この価格でのご提供は今回限りとなります。

We are only able to offer this price once.

値引きに応じますので、長いお付き合いになることを願っています。

We accept your request for a discount and we hope this will lead to a long-term relationship.

その金額で請求書をお送りいただけたらと思います。

I'd appreciate it if you could send me an invoice for that amount.

見積もりの金額で問題ありません。

We're satisfied with the amount you quoted.

協議の結果、総額から5%の値引きが可能になりました。

As a result of the negotiations, a 5 % discount on the total is feasible.

前向きな返信をお待ちしております。

We look forward to a favorable reply.

こちらが弊社が提供可能な最低価格となります。

This is the lowest price we can offer.

新たなお見積もりは追ってお送りいたします。

We'll email you a new quotation.

新たな料金表を添付しましたので、ご確認ください。

Please see the attached revised price list.

7-b 申し出を断る

件名：Re：re：オフィス用品の見積もり

翔太様

この度は先日お送りした見積書へのご連絡ありがとうございます。

あいにく、貴社のご要望にはお応えすることができません。ご期待に添えず大変申し訳ございません。

引き続きご検討いただけましたら幸いです。

よろしくお願いします。
スティーブ

Subject: Re: re: Estimate for office furniture

Dear Shota,

Thank you for your message regarding the estimate I sent the other day.

Unfortunately, we are unable to meet your company's request. We apologize for not being able to fulfill your expectations.

We hope you will consider us again in the future.

Thank you,
Steve

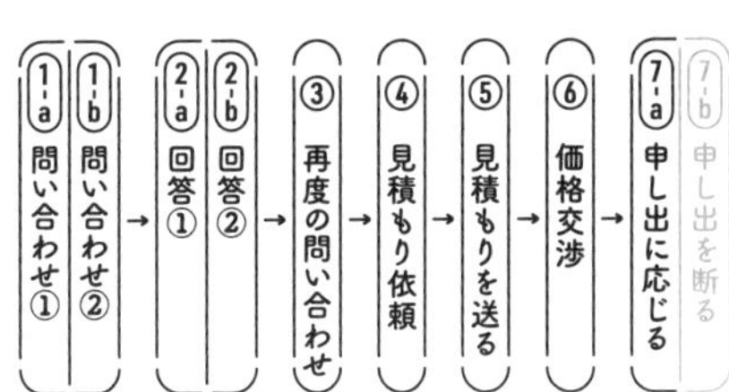

言い換えセンテンス

10%の割引をご希望とのメールを受け取りました。

We have received your email requesting a 10% discount.

見積もり価格にご満足いただけず、残念です。

We are sorry to hear that our estimate was not satisfactory.

お見積もりでご提示した価格は最善のものです。

The price in the estimate is our best offer.

貴社のご要望を検討いたしましたが、あいにくご期待には添えかねます。

We have considered your request, but unfortunately we are unable to satisfy it.

これ以上の値引きはいたしかねます。

We can't offer a lower price.

これ以上お安くはできません。

This is our best price.

1 ユニット 50 ドルが最低価格です。

Our lowest price is $50 per unit.

こちらのサービスは値引きを行っておりません。

We do not offer discounts for this service.

納期はこれ以上前倒しにできません。

We can't deliver it any sooner than this.

残念ながら弊社は商品の値引きをしておりません。

Unfortunately, we do not offer discounts on our items.

送料の高騰(とう)により、配送費は値引きできかねます。

We are unable to offer a discount on delivery fees due to rising shipping costs.

弊社の価格は決して高いものではございません。

Our company's price is very competitive.

1,000 個以上ご注文いただけたら 5%の値引きが可能です。

A 5% discount is available for an order of 1,000 units or more.

お送りした見積もりは、最大限の努力をした金額です。

Our quote is the best offer we can make.

ご期待に添えず残念です。

We regret that we were unable to fulfill your expectations.

貴社のことを大変重要な顧客と考えております。

We greatly value your company as a customer.

それでもご注文いただける際はお知らせください。

Let us know if you are still interested in going forward with your order.

ご理解いただけましたら幸いです。

Your understanding would be greatly appreciated.

PART 1
社外とのやりとり

CHAPTER 7
発注・出荷

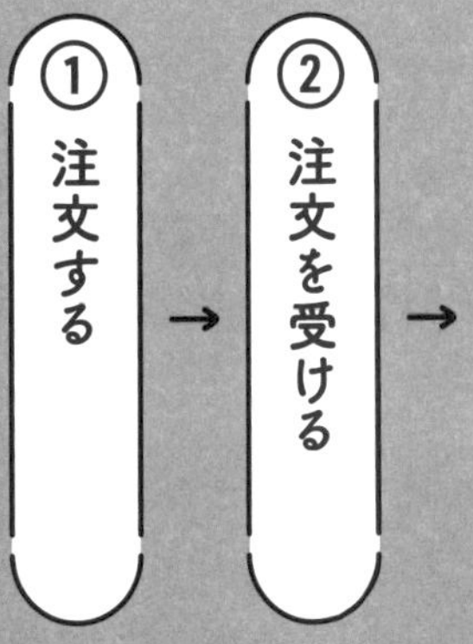

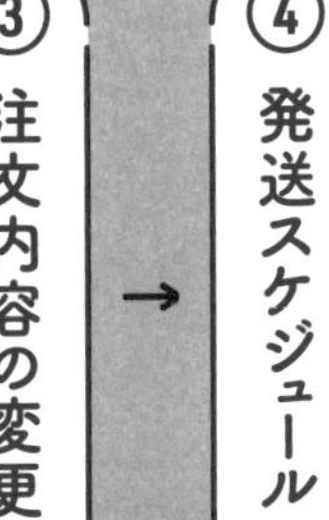

④
発送スケジュール

⑤
スケジュールの変更

① 注文する

件名：タイルの注文

ビル様

下記の品を注文いたします。
・商品：床タイル
・モデル：78BDS
・色：茶色
・数量：46,800 枚

納品は 6 月 14 日から 16 日までの間にお願いします。問題があればお知らせください。ご連絡をお待ちしております。

よろしくお願いします。
鈴木真衣

Subject: Order for tiles

Dear Bill,

We would like to place the following order:
Product: Floor tiles
Model: 78BDS
Color: Brown
Qty.: 46,800 tiles

We would like the order delivered between June 14-16. Please let me know if this will be a problem. We look forward to hearing from you.

Sincerely,
Mai Suzuki

言い換えセンテンス

以下を弊社からの正式な注文としてください。

The following is our official order:

納品は 6 月 10 日から 16 日までの間にお願いします。

We need the order delivered between June 10-16.

この期限に間に合わないようでしたら本日中にお知らせください。

Please notify me by today if this deadline is not possible.

正式な注文書を添付いたしました。

An official order form is included.

早めにこの注文を処理していただけますか？

Would it be possible to process this order quickly?

オンライン決済ですでに支払いを終えています。

We've already made our payment through your site.

着払いで送ってください。

Please send our order POD.

payment on delivery で「着払い」を意味する。

支払い方法を教えてください。

Please let me know about the payment method.

領収書を同封していただけますか？

Please make sure you enclose the receipt.

領収書の宛名は弊社で、項目は「品代」でお願いします。

Please write our company name on the receipt and list the items as "commodities."

なるべく早めの発送をお願いします。

Please ship it as soon as possible.

最短での発送をお願いします。

Please use the fastest shipping method.

発送のめどが立ちましたらお知らせください。

Please let us know when you plan to send the order.

到着のめどが立ちましたら教えてください。

Please let us know when we can expect to receive our order.

船便 / 航空便 / 翌日配達で配送してください。

Please send our order by sea/by airmail/by overnight express.

商品の発送後にご連絡をお願いいたします。

Could you please let us know once the order has been shipped?

ご連絡をお待ちしています。

We're looking forward to hearing from you.

ご協力いただきありがとうございます。

Thank you for your cooperation.

値引きに応じていただきありがとうございました。

Thank you for the discount.

② 注文を受ける

件名：Re：タイルの注文

真衣様

タイル 46,800 枚のご注文を承りました。発送の手続きを開始するのに必要な情報はすべてそろいました。

何か問題が生じましたら、直ちにご連絡いたします。

ありがとうございます。
ビル

Subject: Re: Order for tiles

Dear Mai,

We have received your order for 46,800 tiles. We now have all the information we need to start processing your shipment.

If any problems arise, I will contact you immediately.

Many thanks,
Bill

①注文する → ②注文を受ける → ③注文内容の変更 → ④発送スケジュール → ⑤スケジュールの変更

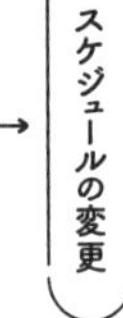

言い換えセンテンス

46,800 枚のタイルのご注文、ありがとうございます。

Thank you for your order for 46,800 tiles.

ご注文ありがとうございます。

Thank you for your order.

ご注文をいただき出荷手続きを開始いたしました。

We have received and started processing your shipment.

必要な情報をすべてお送りいただけましたので注文の処理を開始します。

We have all the information needed, so we'll begin processing your order.

ご注文の処理を進める前に 1 点確認したいことがあります。

Before we start processing your order, I'd like to clarify one thing.

今から数日以内にご注文の品を出荷いたします。

We should be able to ship your order within a few days.

配送スケジュールが確定したらご連絡いたします。
I'll let you know as soon as the shipping schedule is finalized.

配達予定時刻は 5 月 5 日の午後 5 時です。
The estimated arrival time is 5:00 p.m. on May 5.

順調にいけば、来月上旬には発送する予定です。
If everything goes as expected, we'll be able to ship your order early next month.

何か問題が起こりましたらすぐにご連絡いたします。
If we encounter any problems, I'll let you know right away.

この度はお買い上げいただき誠にありがとうございました。
Thank you very much for your purchase.

至急手配します。
We'll take care of this right away.

追加のご注文などあれば、1 月 15 日（金）までにメールをください。
If you'd like to place an additional order, please email me by Friday, January 15.

ご注文確認後にメールを送ります。
I'll email you after I verify your order.

最終的な承認をいただければ、ご注文の品を発送いたします。

If you could give us your final approval, we'll ship your order.

いつも取引をしていただき、ありがとうございます。

Thank you as always for doing business with us.

商品到着までもうしばらくお待ちください。

We need to ask you to wait a little longer for your order.

③ 注文内容の変更

件名：注文変更のお願い（No. 4421）

リチャード様

申し訳ありませんが、昨日弊社が送った注文を変更する必要があります。部品を 5,500 個ではなく、5,600 個注文したいと思います（342 モデル）。

可能でしたら変更後の請求額の合計をお知らせいただけますでしょうか？

よろしくお願いします。
マイ

Subject: Request to revise order (No. 4421)

Hi Richard,

I'm afraid we need to change the order we sent to you yesterday. Instead of 5,500 parts (Model 342), we'd like to order 5,600.

If this is possible, could you send me the revised total balance due?

Thanks for your help,
Mai

言い換えセンテンス

まだ注文の変更はできますか？

Is it still possible to change my order?

変更はいつまで可能ですか？

What's the deadline for change?

注文数を増やすこと／減らすことは可能ですか？

Is it possible to increase/decrease the size of my order?

製品番号が間違っていたので変更したいです。

The product number was incorrect, so I'd like to correct it.

もし手遅れでなければ注文を変更したいです。

We need to change our order, if it's not too late.

注文数を 5,500 個から 5,600 個に増やしていただけるようお願いします。

We'd like to ask you to increase our order from 5,500 to 5,600 parts.

弊社の注文数は 5,500 個でしたが、これを 5,400 個に減らしたいと思います（342 モデル）。

Our order was for 5,500 parts (Model 342), but we'd like to decrease this to 5,400 parts.

もしむずかしければ、すぐにお知らせいただけますか？

If this is not possible, could you let me know right away?

これが可能なのかどうか、また新しい総額がいくらになるか教えていただけますか？

Could you let me know if this is possible, and also what the new total cost will be?

変更を知らせていただきありがとうございます。

Thanks for letting us know about this change.

ご注文の変更は何の問題もございません。

It won't be any problem at all to revise the order for you.

参考までに変更後の請求書を添付いたしました。

I've attached a revised invoice for your reference.

変更はまだ間に合います。

I'm happy to inform you that it is not too late to make this change.

残念ですが、変更できる日にちを過ぎています。

I'm afraid it is too late to make changes.

残念ですが、弊社ではこの依頼に対応することはできません。

Unfortunately, we are unable to accommodate this request.

他にも何かあれば遠慮なくお知らせください。

Please feel free to let us know if you need anything else.

④ 発送スケジュール

件名：発送スケジュール（請求書 4566）

鈴木様

こちらが提案したい出荷スケジュールは以下の通りです。

1月15日：第1便をアメリカ工場より発送
1月20日：第2便をアメリカ工場より発送

注文の品は2回に分けて出荷したほうがコスト安になります。もし、一度に出荷することをご希望でしたらお知らせください。

よろしくお願いいたします。
ビル・マーティン

Subject: Shipping schedule (Invoice 4566)

Dear Suzuki-san,

We would like to propose the following shipment schedule:

January 15: 1st shipment from US plant
January 20: 2nd shipment from US plant

It will cost less to send the order in two shipments, but please let me know if you'd like everything sent in one shipment.

Best wishes,
Bill Martin

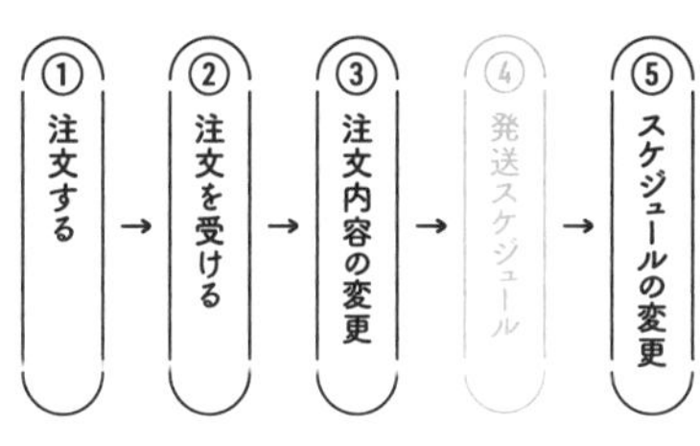

言い換えセンテンス

発送のスケジュールが決まりましたのでお知らせします。

This is to let you know that the shipping schedule has been finalized.

現在ご注文いただいた商品の手配をしておりますので、確保でき次第発送いたします。

We are currently procuring the items in your order, and we will ship them as soon as we get everything.

ご注文の品は 10 月 29 日に発送の予定です。

Your order is scheduled to be shipped on October 29.

発送は明日を予定しておりましたが、2、3 日遅延してしまいそうです。

We are planning to ship tomorrow, but it seems that it will be delayed for a few days.

現在、倉庫から商品を取り寄せていますので、あと 2 週間ほどかかります。

We are currently getting the product from our warehouse, so it will take approximately two more weeks.

アメリカから日本に送る時にかかる関税が 100 ドルで、送料の合計は 350 ドルです。こちらを請求書へ記入しておいてください。

The tariff on shipments from the US to Japan is $100 for a total shipment charge of $350. Please include this figure in the invoice.

新たな発送スケジュールは以下の通りになります。

Here is the new shipping schedule:

船便の手配が済み次第、詳細をお知らせいたします。

We will inform you of the details as soon as shipping has been arranged.

注文の品は本日朝 10 時に工場より出荷されました。

Your order left the factory this morning at 10:00.

すべてが順調に進めば、3 日以内に届くはずです。

If everything goes smoothly, it should arrive within three days.

---

7 月 10 日の午前中指定の宅配便で、商品を発送いたしました。

Your order was sent by courier and is scheduled to arrive on the morning of July 10.

ABC 船会社の BBB という船がアムステルダム港を 10 月 20 日に出港、12 月 1 日に東京に到着予定です。

An ABC ship called BBB will depart Amsterdam Port on October 20 and arrive in Tokyo on December 1.

船便の到着が遅れそうだと運送業者から連絡がありました。

The forwarder has informed me that the order being sent by sea will be delayed.

問題があればお知らせください。

Please let me know if this will be a problem.

航空便で送りました。12 月 8 日に配送予定です。

I sent it by airmail, and it will be delivered on December 8.

FedEx で以下の住所に請求書を送りました。追跡番号は以下の通りです。

I sent an invoice to the below address by FedEx. The tracking number is as follows:

請求書の原本は配送物に入っております。

The original invoice is included in the shipment.

予定日を過ぎても届かない場合はご一報ください。

If you do not receive it as scheduled, please let me know.

⑤ スケジュールの変更

件名：注文番号 123 の配送日が 12 月 2 日から 9 日に変更になりました

翔太様

残念ながら到着日の変更をお伝えする必要があります。

当初は 12 月 2 日に東京着の予定だったのですが、12 月 9 日の到着予定になります。

ご迷惑をおかけして申し訳ありません。

よろしくお願いします。
アレックス

Subject: Order 123: delivery date changed from December 2 to December 9

Hello Shota,

I'm afraid I need to inform you of a change in the arrival date.

The order was originally scheduled to arrive in Tokyo on December 2, but we have been informed that it will arrive on December 9.

I apologize for the inconvenience.

Thanks,
Alex

言い換えセンテンス

こちらの手違いで配送日が遅れてしまいました。

Due to an error on our side the delivery date has been delayed.

注文番号 12345 について遅延が発生していることをお知らせします。

We need to let you know that your order (No. 12345) will be delayed.

流通の都合で、当初の出荷スケジュールよりも 1 週間遅れそうです。

Due to shipping problems, shipments are about one week behind schedule.

当初の予定よりも早く出荷できそうですが、よろしいでしょうか？

It seems that we can ship earlier than originally planned. Would this be preferable for you?

住所不明で注文の品が戻ってきました。

Your order was returned to us because the address was incorrect.

早急に住所をご確認いただけますか？

Could you verify your address as soon as possible?

住所は以下の通りで間違いありませんか？
Could you make sure the address below is correct?

あらためて住所を教えていただけますか？
Could you let us know your address again?

在庫の確保ができなかったため、一旦発送を保留にしております。
We are unable to obtain the items in the order, so the shipment has been put on hold.

船会社が変更となりましたが、到着予定日は変わりません。
The shipping company has changed, but the expected arrival date remains the same.

変更に伴う追加の費用はこちらで負担いたします。
We will cover the additional costs associated with the change.

納品の遅延によりキャンセルをご希望の場合は早めにお知らせください。
If you wish to cancel due to this delivery delay, please let us know as soon as possible.

至急、航空便で送らせていただきます。
We will send it by airmail as soon as possible.

航空便と船便のどちらを希望しますか？
Which do you prefer, airmail or surface mail?

お待たせしてしまい大変申し訳ございません。

We are very sorry to have kept you waiting.

注文の品は間もなく到着する予定です。

Your order will arrive shortly.

ご不便をおかけしますが、どうぞよろしくお願いいたします。

We apologize for any inconvenience.

発送が遅れてしまい誠に申し訳ございません。

Please accept our sincere apologies for the delayed shipment.

PART 1
社外とのやりとり

CHAPTER 8
業務提携・契約

① 業務提携の提案 → 2-a 応じる / 2-b 断る → ③ 契約書の草案 → ④ 草案の内容確認 → ⑤ 契約書の送付 → ⑥ 返送する

① 業務提携の提案

件名：日本での販売代理店の契約について

ご担当者様

弊社は日本でカーケア用品を販売しているABCケアプロという企業です。東京での展示会で、貴社のカーケア用品を試させていただき、ぜひ日本で販売できればと思っています。

日本でこのような製品はまだありませんので、大きなビジネスになると見込んでおります。弊社のウェブサイトは以下の通りです。ご検討いただけたらと思います。

お願いします。
深田まこと

Subject: Japan sales agency contract

To whom it may concern,

Our company, ABC Care Pro, sells car care products in Japan. We tried your company's car care products at an exhibition in Tokyo and decided that we would like to sell them in Japan, if possible.

There are no products like yours in Japan, so we believe this could be a big business opportunity for you. Our company's website is listed below. We appreciate your consideration.

Sincerely,
Makoto Fukada

言い換えセンテンス

お互いの利益になるような業務提携のご提案をさせていただきたく、メールしました。

I'm writing with a business proposal that I believe may be of mutual benefit.

貴社のホームページで代理店募集の記載を見て連絡させていただきました。

I'm contacting you because I saw on your website that you are looking for agents.

弊社の製品を販売していただける代理店を探しております。

We are looking for a distributor to sell our products.

ゼネラル・カーズの宮下さまからのご紹介でメールさせていただきました。

I'm contacting you because I was introduced to you by Mr. Miyashita of General Cars.

弊社は精密機器の部品を製造しているメーカーです。

We manufacture precision instrument parts.

日本での販売をお考えですか？

Are you planning to sell your products in Japan?

貴社の製品の日本における独占販売店として、ご検討いただければ幸いです。

We'd be grateful if you could consider the possibility of appointing us as exclusive distributor for your products in Japan.

アジア地域でのシステム導入を検討されたことはありますか?

Have you considered introducing your system in the Asian region?

他社との技術提携を検討されたことはありますか?

Have you ever considered technical cooperation with other companies?

弊社を販売代理店としてご検討いただけたら幸いです。

We hope you will consider us your sales agent.

貴社の子ども服の日本での独占販売の契約をさせていただきたいと考えております。

We would like to sign an exclusive distribution contract for your children's clothing line in Japan.

コーヒー豆の輸入の契約を貴社と結びたいと思っております。

We wish to enter into a contract with you to import coffee beans.

当社のシステムを導入することで、仕事の効率が劇的に向上します。

We are confident that our system will significantly improve the efficiency of your business.

もし弊社に独占販売の許可をいただけたら、全力でセールスプロモーションを行います。

If we are given exclusive sales rights, we will put all our efforts into promotional activities.

貴社の製品の売上拡大のお手伝いができればと思います。

I would like to help your company expand product sales.

ぜひ、弊社も候補に入れていただきたいと思います。

We hope that you will consider us a candidate.

貴社のお考えを伺えればと思います。

We'd like to know your company's perspective on this.

弊社の詳細についてお会いしてご説明させていただきたいと思います。

I'd like to meet with you in person and tell you more about our company.

2-a 応じる

件名：re：日本での販売代理店契約について

マコト様

ご連絡をいただきありがとうございました。

社内でこの件について確認しました。ぜひ前向きに検討させてください。

今回の提携をきっかけに双方に利益をもたらす関係を築いていきたいです。

ミシェル・アニンストン

Subject: re: Japan distributorship agreement

Dear Makoto,

Thank you for contacting us.

We have reviewed the matter internally and our impression is favorable.

We hope that, through this partnership, we can build a prosperous relationship that would be beneficial for both of our companies.

Michelle Anniston

言い換えセンテンス

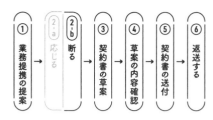

弊社の販売代理店になることに関心をお持ちとのメールを読みました。

We have reviewed your email regarding your company's interest in becoming our distributor.

弊社の製品に興味をお持ちいただきありがとうございます。

Thank you very much for your interest in our products.

日本の販売代理店に興味があります。

We are interested in having a Japanese distributor.

ジョシュ・ローガンからメールの転送を受け取りました。

Josh Rogan has forwarded your email to me.

貴社の提案は大変魅力的です。

We find your proposal very interesting.

貴社のご提案に大変興味があります。慎重に検討します。

We are very interested in your suggestions, and they will be carefully considered.

社内でも話し合い、ぜひ前向きに進めたいという結論に至りました。

We discussed it internally and concluded that we would definitely like to move forward with this.

この件についてさらに話し合いたいです。

We would like to further discuss this matter.

海外での事業拡大を考えております。

We are considering overseas business expansion.

この度はこのようなお申し出をいただき、感激しております。

We are very excited to have received this offer.

貴社からの具体的な案をお待ちしております。

We look forward to receiving a concrete plan from you.

弊社のサービスに興味を持っていただき誠にありがとうございます。

Thank you very much for your interest in our services.

詳細については後日あらためてご連絡させていただきます。

We will contact you again with more details.

いつまでにお返事をすればよろしいでしょうか？

By when would you like us to give you a reply?

正式な話し合いの場を持つことができればと思います。

We would like to arrange a formal discussion.

これが両社の発展のきっかけになることを願っております。

We hope that this will be a catalyst for the further development of our companies.

末長いお付き合いをよろしくお願いいたします。

We look forward to a long-term relationship with you.

2-b 断る

件名：業務提携の申し出について

ナンシー・フォールズ様

この度は、弊社との業務提携をご提案いただきありがとうございました。現時点では海外への進出を考えておりません。せっかくの申し出をお断りすることになり、心苦しい限りです。

弊社の方針が変更になった際には、お声がけをさせていただきます。

鈴木真衣

Subject: Offer for business cooperation

Dear Nancy Falls,

Thank you for your offer to partner with our company. Unfortunately, overseas business expansion is not in our plans at this time. I am very sorry to have to decline your offer.

If our plans do change, we will be sure to contact you again.

Mai Suzuki

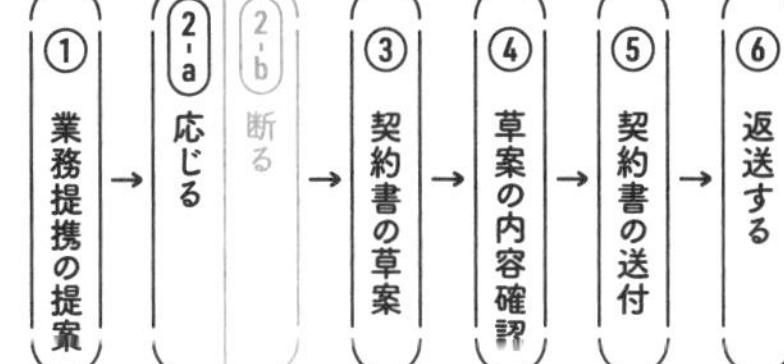

言い換えセンテンス

この度はパートナーとして弊社をご検討いただき、感謝申し上げます。

We would like to thank you for considering us as a partner.

業務提携の申し出、誠にありがとうございます。

Thank you very much for your offer of a business alliance.

販売代理店のご提案ありがとうございました。

Thank you for the offer to serve as our distributor.

残念ですが今回のご提案はお断りさせていただきます。

We are afraid that we must decline your proposal at this time.

社内で検討した結果、今回は申し出をお断りすることになりました。

We have discussed the matter internally and have concluded that we will have to decline your offer.

ご提案を真剣に検討させていただきましたが、辞退することになりました。

We have given your proposal serious consideration but have decided to decline it.

現在のところ、弊社の製品を海外で販売する計画はありません。

At present, we have no plans to sell our products overseas.

弊社には、貴社のビジネスプランに対応できる程の余裕がありません。

We are unable to satisfy the conditions of your business plan.

専売契約を他社と結んでおります。

We have an exclusive sales contract with another company.

別の企業との業務提携が決まったところです。

We have just decided to enter into a business partnership with another company.

今のところ事業を拡大する予定はありません。

We have no plans to expand our business for now.

ありがたい申し出を本当にありがとうございます。

Thank you very much for your kind offer.

今回はご期待に添えず申し訳ありませんが、今後別の形で貴社とお付き合いができたらと思っております。

We are sorry that we cannot work with you on this matter, but we look forward to future opportunities to work together.

貴社の製品／サービスに興味を持ちそうな会社を紹介することも可能です。

We can introduce you to another company that may be interested in your products and services.

ご一緒する機会を楽しみにしております。

We look forward to the opportunity to work with you in the future.

お仕事でご一緒できることを楽しみにしています。

We are looking forward to working with you in the future.

貴社の発展をお祈りしております。

I wish you all the best.

せっかくのご提案にお応えできず、申し訳ございません。

I'm afraid that we are unable to accept your offer.

提案をお断りすることになり、申し訳ありません。

We're sorry to have to turn down your proposal.

③ 契約書の草案

件名：契約書のドラフトです

アレックス様

契約書の草案を添付いたしました。問題がないかご確認いただければと思います。何か問題があれば遠慮なくお知らせください。

必要であれば集まって打ち合わせをすることも可能です。お返事お待ちしております。

山本翔太

Subject: Contract draft

Dear Alex,

I have attached a draft of the contract. Please take a look to see if there are any issues. If there are problems, please don't hesitate to contact me.

We can get together to discuss it if necessary. I look forward to hearing from you.

Shota Yamamoto

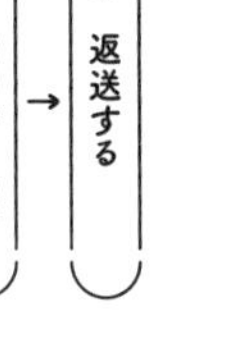

言い換えセンテンス

契約書のドラフトを添付しました。ご確認ください。

Please find attached a draft of the contract for your review.

打ち合わせで話したことを基に契約書の草案を作成いたしました。

We have drafted a contract based on what we talked about at the meeting.

契約書の草案を添付します。

I've attached a draft of the contract.

こちらをたたき台にして契約書を作成できると思います。

Perhaps we could use this as a rough draft for the contract.

添付は契約書の案です。

Attached is a draft of the contract.

契約書のドラフトを作成いたしました。

We have created a draft for the contract.

率直な意見を伺えればと思います。

I would appreciate hearing your frank opinion.

コメントは直接草案に書き込んでいただければと思います。

If you have any comments, I would appreciate it if you could write them directly on the draft.

草案で変更したい点があれば原稿に直接書き込んでご返送ください。

If there are any changes you'd like to make to the draft, please input your revisions directly into the file and return it to us.

草案に問題がなければ、すぐに正式な契約書をお送りします。

Once you have approved the draft, we will send you the formal contract immediately.

今月末までにお返事を頂きたいです。

Please get back to us by the end of this month.

速達で契約書の草案を送らせていただきました。

We have sent a draft of the contract by express mail.

１部を控えとして保管してください。

Please keep one copy for your records.

お待たせして申し訳ありませんでした。

We're sorry to have kept you waiting.

送付に時間がかかってしまい申し訳ありません。

We're sorry we were unable to send it more promptly.

議論の結果を正式なものに反映していきます。

The results of our discussion will be reflected in the official version.

草案を承認いただきありがとうございます。

Thank you for approving the draft.

ご質問があれば、遠慮なくお知らせください。

Please don't hesitate to contact us if you have any questions.

④ 草案の内容確認

件名：契約書に関する質問

アレックス様

先日は契約書の草案を送っていただきありがとうございました。

早速拝見しましたが、質問があります。商品到着後 60 日以内に支払いとありますが間違いないでしょうか？ 弊社は通常、到着後 90 日以内にお支払いをしています。

ご確認ください。

鈴木真衣

Subject: Question about contract

Hi Alex,

Thank you for sending the draft contract the other day.

I read it over and I have a question. It says that the payment deadline is within 60 days of arrival. Is this correct? We usually pay within 90 days of arrival.

Please let me know.

Mai Suzuki

言い換えセンテンス

本日契約書を確かに受け取りました。

I'm confirming that I've received the contract today.

契約書の草案を上司と確認させていただきました。

I confirmed the draft contract with my boss.

いくつか質問がありますので回答いただければと思います。

I have a few questions that I'd like you to answer.

正式に契約を交わす前にいくつか質問させてください。

I'd like to ask you a few questions before we officially sign the contract.

契約書のドラフトのご確認ありがとうございます。

Thank you for confirming the draft contract.

契約書に関する質問をありがとうございました。

Thank you for your questions regarding the contract.

契約書についての質問の回答まで少し時間をください。

Please give me a little time to answer your questions regarding the contract.

この件について経理部に相談する必要がありますので少しお待ちください。

I'll need to discuss this with the accounting department, so please give me a little time.

インセンティブの数字が最初に話した内容と異なるようです。

The incentive figure appears to be different to what we initially discussed.

支払い期日に関してですが、翌月ではなく翌々月にすることは可能ですか？

As for the payment terms, is NET 60 instead of NET 30 possible?

NET 60 = The net amount of the invoice is due 60 days after the invoice date. の略。請求書の日付から 60 日以内に全額を支払う条件を表す。

締め切りがタイトなので少し余裕を持たせることは可能ですか？

The deadline is a little tight, so would it be possible to have some more time?

あいにく契約の内容を変更することはできません。

I'm afraid we can't make any changes to the contract.

契約内容の変更について打ち合わせさせていただけますか？

Would it be possible to have a meeting regarding the contract changes?

違約金について聞いていなかったため、詳しくお話を伺いたいです。

I haven't heard about the contract breach penalties yet, so I'd like to get some more details on that.

今後も末長いお付き合いをお願いします。

We look forward to an ongoing relationship with you.

その点以外は契約書の内容を全て理解しました。

Apart from that, everything regarding the contract makes sense.

何度も質問をしてしまいすみません。

I apologize for all the questions.

何か質問があればお知らせください。電話いたします。

If you have any questions, please let me know and I'll give you a call.

⑤ 契約書の送付

件名：契約書の送付

スティーブ様

契約書を 2 部郵送いたしました。両方に署名してください。1 部はご自分で保管していただき、1 部はご返送ください。

これから一緒にお仕事ができることを楽しみにしております。

ABC 社
山本一郎

Subject: Contract sent

Dear Steve,

I have mailed you two copies of the contract. Please sign both copies, keep one for yourself, and send one signed copy back to us.

We are looking forward to working with you.

Ichiro Yamamoto
ABC Inc.

言い換えセンテンス

先日の会議を基に契約書を作成しました。

I made a contract based on the meeting the other day.

契約書の準備ができました。

The contract is ready.

契約書をご確認いただけますか？

Could you check the contract?

訂正箇所があればお知らせください。

Please let us know if there are any corrections.

契約書ができたので、送らせていただきます。

I have attached the completed contract.

不備がないかご確認ください。

Please check to see if there are any mistakes.

契約書を作成いたしました。

We have drawn up the contract.

契約書に誤りがあればお知らせください。

Please let me know if there are any mistakes in the contract.

問題がないようであれば、署名をお願いします。

Please sign it if everything looks okay.

6 月 15 日までにお返事を頂きたいです。

We'd like to receive a reply by June 15.

速達で契約書を 2 部お送りしました。

We have sent two copies of the contract by express mail.

原本は郵送致しましたので、届かなければお知らせください。

I sent the original by mail. Please let me know if it doesn't arrive.

お待たせしてすみません。

I'm sorry to have kept you waiting.

先日いただいた修正が契約書に反映されているかご確認ください。

Please check to see if the contract reflects the corrections you made the other day.

こちらの認識に間違いがあれば、お知らせください。

Please let me know if I have misunderstood something.

用紙に記入した日付を入力してください。

Please enter the date you filled out the form.

契約書をお待ちしています。

We will look forward to receiving the copies of the contract.

12 月 15 日までに正式な契約を結びたいと思います。

We hope the official contract will be finalized by December 15.

今月末までにご返送いただけたらと思います。

I would appreciate it if you could send it back to me by the end of this month.

⑥ 返送する

件名：Re：契約書の送付

アレックス様

契約書を本日受け取りました。ありがとうございます。内容に問題がないことを確認しました。署名をして１部返送いたします。

貴社との取引が始まり、大変嬉しく思います。末永くお付き合いできることを願っています。

敬具
山本翔太

Subject: Re: Contract sent

Hi Alex,

I received the contract today, thank you very much. I have reviewed the contents and there are no issues. I will sign and return one copy to you.

We are very happy to begin doing business with your company, and we look forward to a long-term relationship.

Sincerely yours,
Shota Yamamoto

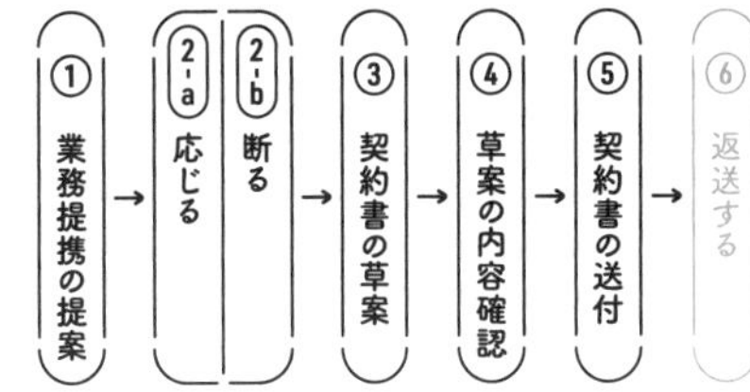

言い換えセンテンス

正式な契約書を 6 月 2 日に受け取りました。

We received the official contract on June 2.

契約書のドラフトを受け取りました。

I have received the draft of the contract.

契約書を早急に手配していただきありがとうございました。

Thank you for your prompt arrangement of the copies of the contract.

上司に確認しましたが、問題ありません。

I've confirmed with my supervisor that there are no issues.

確認したところ、間違いが 1 箇所見つかりました。

I've reviewed it and found one error.

2 部に署名して、先ほど発送いたしました。

I signed two copies and have just sent them out.

2、3 日でそちらに届くと思います。

You should receive it in a couple of days.

署名の前に1点確認したいことがあります。

There is one thing I would like to confirm before signing.

修正をお願いした点が反映されていないようです。

It seems that the changes we requested have not been included.

なるべく早めにご返送します。

We will return it to you as soon as we can.

発送次第メールいたします。

I will email you once I have sent it.

返送の準備が整い次第またご連絡します。

We will contact you again when we are ready to return it to you.

届かない場合は早急にご連絡ください。

If you do not receive it, please contact us immediately.

1部は弊社で保管しています。

We will retain one copy.

2部とも署名しましたので、うち1部をお送りします。

We have signed both copies, and I'm sending you one of them.

これが長いお付き合いの始まりになることを願っています。

We hope that this will be the beginning of a long-term relationship.

両社のさらなる発展のために、協力し合っていければと思います。

We hope that our cooperation will lead to the further growth of our companies.

今後は貴社のパートナーとして尽力させていただきます。

As your company's partner, we will do our best.

PART 1
社外とのやりとり

CHAPTER 9
売り込み

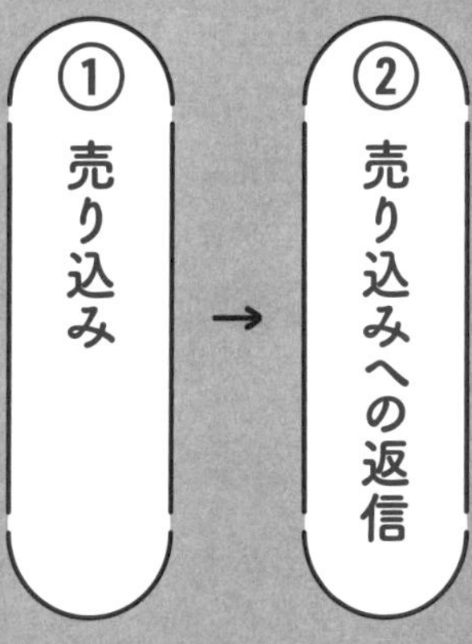

① 売り込み

件名：弊社のアプリに関するご提案

ご担当者様

ABC 社で営業をしておりますリンダ・ウィルソンと申します。

貴社のウェブサイトを拝見し、弊社の開発したアプリがお役に立てるのではないかと思い、ご連絡いたしました。導入することで社内のコミュニケーションが円滑に運びます。興味をお持ちであれば、直接ご説明にお伺いしたく、ご連絡しました。

ご連絡お待ちしております。

よろしくお願いします。
リンダ・ウィルソン

Subject: A proposal regarding our company's app

To whom it may concern,

My name is Linda Wilson and I work in sales at ABC Co.

I am writing to you after I looked at your website and realized that one of our apps might be of use to you. The app can help to ensure smooth communication within your company. If you are interested, I would like to visit you at your convenience to talk about it.

I look forward to hearing from you.

Best regards,
Linda Wilson

言い換えセンテンス

ABCインターナショナル社のリンダ・ウィルソンと申します。

My name is Linda Wilson from ABC International.

弊社は小規模ながら、自動車用の高精度な金属部品を作り成長を続けているメーカーです。

We are a small but growing manufacturer that makes high-precision metal parts for automobiles.

弊社は現在、貴国で弊社の市場拡大のお手伝いをしていただける代理店を探しています。

We're now looking for an agent in your country to help us expand our market.

弊社と定期的に取引をすることにご興味はありますか？

Would you be interested in working with us as a regular supplier?

弊社が提供するアプリはIT業界のお客様を中心に多数導入いただいております。

Our company's apps are used by many companies, mainly in the IT field.

課題解決に役立てていただいた実績がございます。

It has proven to be useful for problem solving in the past.

貴社の材料費削減にどれだけお役に立てるかお話しできたらと思います。

I'd like to let you know how we can help you reduce your material costs.

弊社は塗料および染料を低価格で提供していることで知られています。

We are known for our competitive prices on paints and dyes.

弊社は出版業界における最大手です。

We are the largest company in the publishing industry.

弊社の提案するソリューションは、貴社のコスト削減に大きく貢献することができます。

I'm confident that our solutions can help to greatly reduce your costs.

貴社のコスト削減に大きく貢献できる具体的な案を、ぜひご提案したいと思っています。

We look forward to showing you specific ways we can drastically cut your costs.

最先端の新製品について、ぜひお会いしてお話させていただければと考えています。

We'd greatly appreciate the opportunity to meet with you and talk about our new cutting-edge products.

来週のどこかで 30 分お時間をいただければ、Zoom で弊社の商品についてご説明いたします。

Please let me know if you have 30 minutes anytime next week so I can explain our products on Zoom.

ご都合のよいときにぜひ一度お会いして、弊社がいかにお役に立てるかお話できればと思っています。

I'd like to visit you at a time convenient for you to discuss how my company can be of service to you.

ご興味がおありでしたら、3 月末までにご連絡をいただけますでしょうか？

If you are interested, could you please contact me by the end of March?

お返事お待ちしております。

I'm looking forward to hearing from you.

弊社のビジネスの詳細につきましては、ホームページをご覧ください。

Please visit our site to learn more about our business.

参考までに詳細を添付しました。

I've attached the details for your reference.

② 売り込みへの返信

件名：Re：アプリに関するご提案

リンダ様

アプリに関するご提案ありがとうございます。

貴社のサービスにとても関心があります。一度オンラインで詳しいお話をお聞かせください。日程の候補をいくつかお送りいたします。

3月10日：終日
3月11日：午前中
3月14日：10：00～

都合のつく日をお知らせください。この度はご提案、誠にありがとうございます。

よろしくお願いいたします。
鈴木真衣

Subject: Re: A proposal regarding our company's app

Dear Linda,

Thank you for the proposal regarding your company's app.

I am very interested in your company's services. I'd like to discuss the details with you online if possible. I've listed a couple of possible dates below:

March 10: All day
March 11: Morning
March 14: From 10:00

Let me know if any of these dates work for you. Thank you again for your proposal.

Best regards,
Mai Suzuki

言い換えセンテンス

プリンターのインクの供給についてご連絡をいただき、誠にありがとうございました。

Thank you for contacting us regarding the supply of printer ink.

私たちと取引することに関心を持っていただき、感謝いたします。

We appreciate your interest in working with us.

貴社と取引させていただくことに大変関心を持っております。

We are very much interested in working with you.

貴社のことをよく存じ上げており、大変よい評判を聞いております。

We are familiar with your company, and we know that you have a good reputation.

貴社のサービスにとても興味があります。

We are very interested in your company's services.

サービスの内容や料金体系などについて詳しく知りたいです。

I would like to know more about your services and pricing plan.

よろしければ、この件についてさらに話し合うために弊社の担当者が貴社に伺うことも可能です。

If you'd like, we can send a representative to your office to discuss this matter further.

現時点では、当社では新たなサービスの導入予定はございません。

We have no plans to introduce a new service at the current time.

近々お会いすることはできますか？

Would it be possible to meet in person sometime soon?

一度ご担当者様からお電話をいただくことは可能ですか？

Could the person in charge please give me a call?

残念ですが現時点では、そのようなサービスを導入する予定はありません。

Unfortunately, we do not have plans to use such a service at this time.

あいにくそのようなサービスのための予算がなく、今回のお話はお受けできません。

As we don't currently have the budget for that kind of service, I'm afraid we can't accept your offer.

価格がこちらの予算を上回っているので残念ですがお断りします。

Your price is over our budget, and so I'm afraid we'll have to decline.

あいにく現在弊社はそのようなサービスを求めていません。

Unfortunately, our company does not require such a service at this time.

折り返しのご連絡をお待ちしております。

I look forward your reply.

今回お取引ができず残念ですが、またの機会を楽しみにしております。

I'm sorry we couldn't do business this time, but I look forward to the next opportunity.

提案のご連絡ありがとうございます。

Thank you for contacting us regarding the proposal.

追って担当の者から連絡をさせます。

I will have the person in charge contact you soon.

PART 1
社外とのやりとり

CHAPTER 10
支払い

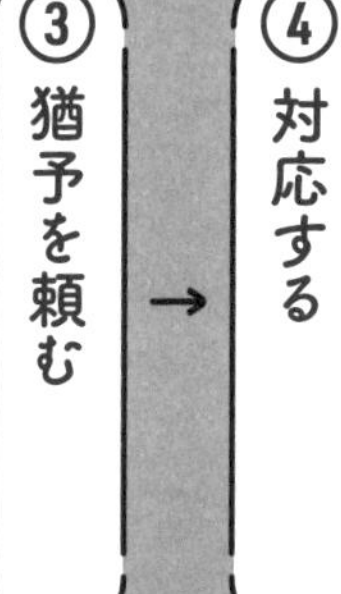
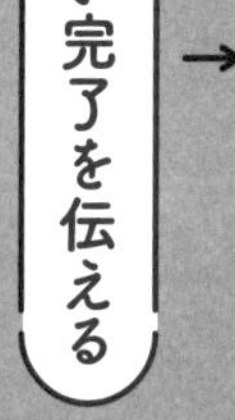

①代金を請求する → ②督促する → ③猶予を頼む → ④対応する → ⑤支払い完了を伝える → ⑥入金の確認を伝える

① 代金を請求する

件名：27 型 2,000 個の請求書

鈴木様

ご依頼いただいた請求書を添付します。総額は 56,000 ドルとなります。
何か不明な点があれば、おっしゃってください。

あらためてお礼を申し上げます。
エレン

Subject: Invoice for 2,000 parts (Model 27)

Suzuki-san,

I have attached the invoice you requested. The total amount comes to $56,000. Please let me know if you have any questions.

Thank you again,
Ellen

言い換えセンテンス

ご依頼いただいた請求書を添付いたします。
I've attached the invoice you requested.

注文番号 12345 の請求書を送らせていただきます。
I am sending the invoice for order 12345.

5 月分の請求書を添付しました。
I have attached the invoice for May.

請求書に不備がないか、ご確認ください。
Please make sure the invoice is in order.

請求額は見積もりと同じ金額です。
The billed amount is the same as the estimate.

もしその方がよければ郵送で請求書を送ることができます。
We can send the invoice by regular mail if you'd prefer.

振り込み先は以下の通りです。
Here is our bank information.

金額に間違いがないかご確認ください。
Please make sure the amount is correct.

請求書に不備があればすぐにお知らせください。
Please let us know right away if this invoice is incomplete.

振込先の情報は請求書に記載されています。
The bank information is listed on the invoice.

10 月 31 日までにお支払いいただけたらと思います。
I would be grateful if you could send the payment by October 31.

なるべく商品到着後 1 カ月以内にお振り込みください。
If possible, please send the payment within one month after the item arrives.

振り込みが完了したらご一報いただけると助かります。
We would appreciate it if you could let us know when the transfer is completed.

いつ頃のお振込みになるか分かればお知らせください。
Please let us know when you plan to make the transfer.

請求書に関して疑問があれば私宛てにメールをください。
Please email me if you have any questions about the invoice.

またのご利用をお待ちしております。

We look forward to serving you again.

この度はご注文ありがとうございました。

Thank you for your order.

今後ともお取引をよろしくお願いいたします。

We look forward to doing business with you again.

② 督促する

件名：8 月注文分の支払いについて

ジェン様

当方の記録によれば、254 番の請求書のお支払いをまだいただいておりません。

もしすでに手続きが済んでいましたら大変申し訳ありません。

ご連絡をお待ちしております。
山田武志

Subject: Payment for August order

Dear Jen,

Our records show that we haven't received your payment for Invoice 254.

I apologize if you have already taken care of this.

Hope to hear from you soon,
Takeshi Yamada

①代金を請求する → ②督促する → ③猶予を頼む → ④対応する → ⑤支払い完了を伝える → ⑥入金の確認を伝える

言い換えセンテンス

お支払いに関するご連絡です。

I'm writing to you regarding payment.

注文番号 12345 のお支払いの件でメールをしました。

I wrote you an email regarding payment for order 12345.

こちらの記録によると、254 番の請求書の支払いがまだ済んでいません。

According to our records, we haven't received your payment for Invoice 254.

弊社の経理部から、先月のお支払いをまだいただいていないという連絡がありました。

Our accounting department has informed me that we have not received last month's payment yet.

5 月 1 日現在、3 月のお支払いをいただいておりません。

As of May 1, we have not received your payment for March.

5 月 20 日正午までにはお振り込みをお願いします。

Please make your payment before 12:00 noon on May 20.

継続して割引サービスを受けるにはお支払いが必要です。

You must pay in order to continue receiving a discount.

もし20日までにお支払いいただくことが不可能であれば、本日中に私にお電話ください。

If you cannot pay by the 20th, please call me by the end of the day.

この件について至急ご確認いただけますでしょうか？

Could you check on this as soon as possible?

大至急お支払いください。

Please complete payment immediately.

念の為、ご請求書を添付いたします。

I'm attaching an invoice for your convenience.

お支払いはいつ頃になりますでしょうか？

When do you think you'll be able to complete the payment?

お支払いのめどは立っておりますでしょうか？

Do you know when you'll be able to complete the payment?

行き違いがございましたらご容赦ください。

I'm sorry if there has been a miscommunication.

すぐに確認できず申し訳ありません。

We apologize for not confirming this sooner.

お支払いの期限は厳守でよろしくお願いいたします。

Please be sure to adhere to the payment schedule.

③ 猶予を頼む

件名：請求書番号 1234 の支払いについて

ノア・ジョーンズ様

支払いが滞っており、誠に申し訳ありません。

クライアントからの支払いが遅延しており、期日を 1 カ月延ばしていただけると大変助かります。

このようなお願いをするのは心苦しいのですが、ご検討いただければ幸いです。

よろしくお願いします
鈴木真衣

Subject: Regarding the payment for invoice 1234

Dear Mr. Noah Jones,

I sincerely apologize for the delay in payment.

We have not received a payment from our client yet, so we would be very grateful if you could extend the deadline by one month.

I apologize for making such a request, but I would appreciate it if you would consider it.

Sincerely,
Mai Suzuki

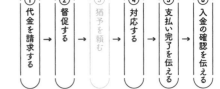

言い換えセンテンス

先月分の支払いが滞っており、誠に申し訳ございません。

I sincerely apologize for the delay in last month's payment.

弊社からの支払いが遅れているとのメールを拝見しました。

I read the email regarding the delay in payment from our company.

支払いの遅延について確認したところ、こちらのミスで滞っていることが分かりました。

After confirming the delay in payment, we found out that the delay was caused by a mistake on our side.

経理のハドソン様より請求書番号 12345 番の注文書の支払い催促のご連絡をいただきました。

I received a reminder from Mr. Hudson from Accounting regarding the payment for invoice 12345.

こちらの手違いで支払い処理がきちんとできておりませんでした。

We couldn't process the payment due to a mistake on our part.

今週中にはお支払いいたしますので少々お待ちください。

I will send the payment this week, so please wait just a little while longer.

できれば数日以内に、なるべく早くお支払いいたします。

I will send the payment as soon as I can, hopefully within a few days.

すぐに代金の一部をお支払いいたしますので、残りはもう少し猶予をいただけますでしょうか?

I will send part of the payment soon, so could I possibly have a little more time to send the remainder?

請求書の手続きが止まっていたことが分かりました。

We discovered that the invoice procedure had stopped.

送金手続きを行いますので、数日ご猶予をいただけたら助かります。

I would appreciate it if I could have a few more days to handle the money transfer procedure.

このようなことは二度とないとお約束いたします。

I promise that something like this will never happen again.

今回に限りご容赦いただけると助かります。

I would appreciate it if you could forgive me just this one time.

図々しいお願いをして大変申し訳ございません。

I'm very sorry for asking such a big favor.

事情をご理解いただけると大変助かります。

I greatly appreciate your understanding of the situation.

これからは必ず期日内に支払うようにいたします。

I will make sure to pay on time from now on.

わがままを申し上げて申し訳ございません。

I'm sorry for being selfish.

当社の手違いで大変ご迷惑をおかけし誠に申し訳ございません。

I'm terribly sorry for all of the trouble our company's mistake has caused.

これに懲(こ)りず、これからも弊社とお取引いただければ幸いです。

I hope this will not discourage business between our two companies in the future.

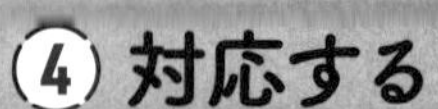

④ 対応する

件名：Re：請求書番号 1234 の支払いについて

真衣様

支払い延期についての連絡をいただきありがとうございます。

貴社の事情は理解できました。１カ月後のお支払いをお待ちしています。

よろしくお願いいたします。
ノア・ジョーンズ

Subject: Re: Regarding the payment for invoice 1234

Dear Mai,

Thank you for your message regarding the delay in payment.

I understand your company's situation. I look forward to receiving your payment in one month.

Best regards,
Noah Jones

言い換えセンテンス

メッセージを読み、事情はよく分かりました。

I saw your message and I understand the situation.

今月末までであれば支払いの期限を延ばせます。

I can extend the payment deadline until the end of this month.

事情は理解できましたが、残念ながら支払いの延期はできません。

I understand your situation, but unfortunately I can't extend the payment deadline.

大変申し訳ないのですが、これ以上の支払い期日の延期は、弊社にとっても非常に厳しいです。

I'm terribly sorry, but it would be very difficult for our company to extend the payment deadline any further.

遅延の理由をお知らせいただきありがとうございました。

Thank you for letting me know the reason for the delay.

数日以内にお支払いいただけるとのご連絡を誠にありがとうございます。

Thank you very much for letting me know that you will pay within a few days.

事情は分かりますが当初の予定通りの期日までにお支払いをお願いしたいと思います。

I understand your situation, but I would like to ask you to pay by the date we originally discussed.

次回のご注文時にお支払いいただけます。

You can pay when you place your next order.

大変申し訳ありませんが、支払い期日の延長はできかねます。

I'm terribly sorry, but we cannot extend the payment deadline.

一部お支払いいただければ、期日の延長に応じます。

We are able to extend the deadline if you can provide a partial.

お支払いのめどが立ちましたら、お知らせください。

Please inform me once you know when the payment is likely to be made.

貴社にはいつも大変お世話になっておりますので、今回に限り支払い期限の延長に同意いたします。

Our two companies have such a good relationship, so I will agree to extending the payment deadline just this once.

契約書に明記しているように期日内にご入金をお願いいたします。

Please pay by the deadline as stipulated in our contract.

ご入金の完了をよろしくお願いいたします。
Please complete the payment.

ご希望に添えず大変申し訳ございません。
I'm terribly sorry for not meeting your request.

それ以上の延期はできませんので、お支払いをお願いいたします。
I am unable to extend the deadline any further, so please complete the payment.

融通が利かず申し訳ありません。
I'm sorry we are unable to be more flexible.

ご返信お待ちしております。
I look forward to your reply.

⑤ 支払い完了を伝える

件名：支払い完了（No. ABC 456）

こんにちは。

たった今、部品「342 モデル」5,500 個分の支払いを行いました。24 時間以内に総額（24,660 ドル）が貴社の口座に振り込まれていることをご確認いただけるはずです。

何かご質問がありましたら、お知らせください。

ありがとうございます。
真衣

Subject: Payment completed (No. ABC 456)

Hi,

We just sent the payment for 5,500 parts (Model 342). You should be able to verify within 24 hours that the total ($24,660) has been deposited into your account.

Please let me know if you have any questions.

Thanks,
Mai

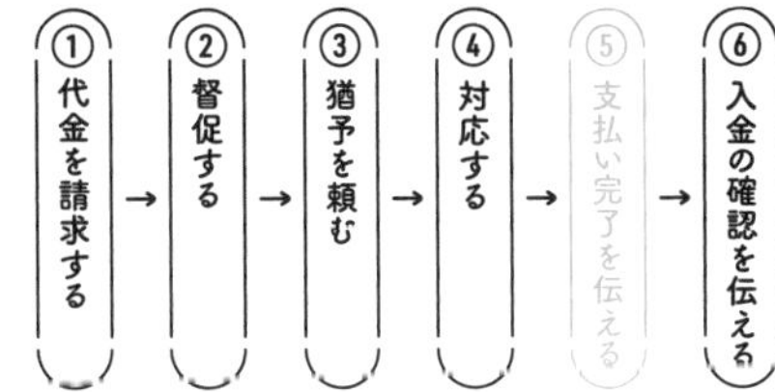

言い換えセンテンス

5月分の請求書をありがとうございました。

Thank you for sending us the invoice for May.

支払い手続きは完了しました。

The payment process has been completed.

もし支払いが確認できなければ、お知らせください。

Please let us know if you are unable to verify the payment.

1点だけご質問させてください。

I'd like to ask you about just one thing.

この点以外は問題ありません。

Everything looks okay except this.

金額を確認させてください。

I'd like to verify the amount.

合計金額が間違っているようですので、訂正して改訂版をお送りください。

The total seems to be incorrect, so please correct it and send us the revised documentation.

支払い方法について教えていただけませんか？
Could you inform me of the payment method?

次回の注文時に今回の注文分とまとめて支払うことは可能ですか？
Would it be possible to pay for this order together with our next order?

海外送金の手続きが完了しました。
The overseas remittance procedure has been completed.

記録が反映されるまで数日かかると思います。
It might take a few days to appear in your records.

明日には入金の確認が取れると思います。
We should be able to confirm the payment tomorrow.

弊社の支払いの確認が取れない場合は、至急ご連絡ください。
If you're not able to confirm our payment, please email me immediately.

ネットバンクの口座をお持ちですか？
Do you have an internet bank account?

ご確認をお願いできますか？
Could you please look into this?

全額支払われているという認識です。

It is our understanding that the payment has now been made in full.

支払いに関して疑問があれば、経理部までご連絡ください。

Please ask our accounting department directly if you have any questions about the payments.

何かご不明でしたら、お知らせください。

If anything is unclear, please let me know.

⑥ 入金の確認を伝える

件名：入金を確認しました

アレックス様

さきほど、入金を確認いたしましたことをお知らせいたします。今後も弊社とのお取引をどうぞよろしくお願いいたします。

お願いします
山本翔太

Subject: Payment verified

Dear Alex,

I'd like to let you know that we have verified receipt of payment. We look forward to working with you in the future.

Best wishes,
Shota Yamamoto

言い換えセンテンス

ご入金いただきありがとうございました。

Thank you for your payment.

12345 番の請求書のお支払いのご連絡ありがとうございます。

Thank you for your email regarding the payment of invoice No. 12345.

ご入金の確認が取れました。

We have verified the payment.

貴社からのお支払いを本日拝受いたしました。

Your payment has been received today.

貴社のお支払いを確認いたしました。すべてが整っているようです。

Your payment has been verified, and everything appears to be in order.

お支払いが確認できましたことを喜んでお知らせいたします。

I'm happy to inform you that your payment has been verified.

残念ですが貴社のお支払いが確認できませんでした。

I'm afraid I was not able to verify your payment.

5月1日の時点でお支払いの確認が取れておりません。

Payment has not been confirmed as of May 1.

残金は2月22日までにお支払いください。

Please pay the remainder by February 22.

入金確認のご連絡が遅くなり申し訳ありません。

We apologize for the delay in contacting you regarding the confirmation of payment.

もし商品が5月12日までに到着しない場合はお知らせいただけますか？

If the product doesn't arrive by May 12, could you let me know?

残金はなるべく早めにお支払いいただけたら助かります。

I would appreciate it if you could pay the remainder as soon as possible.

領収書が必要でしたらお申しつけください。

If you need a receipt, please let us know.

領収書は郵便でお送りいたします。

We will send a receipt to you by mail.

いつも速やかなご入金ありがとうございます。

Thank you as always for your prompt payment.

速やかなご入金をありがとうございました。

Thank you for paying in a prompt manner.

この度はご注文ありがとうございました。

Thank you for your order.

またのご注文をお待ちしております。

We are looking forward to your next order.

PART 1
社外とのやりとり

CHAPTER 11
クレーム

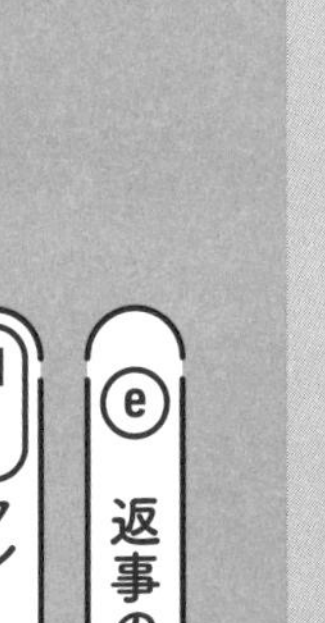

- a-1 クレーム（納期）→ a-2 クレーム対応
- b-1 クレーム（誤発送）→ b-2 クレーム対応
- c-1 クレーム（不良品・欠品）→ c-2 クレーム対応
- d-1 クレーム（サービス）→ d-1 クレーム対応
- e 返事の催促

a-1 クレーム（納期）

件名：Re：注文した20台のノートパソコンについて

ブラウン様

今回、そちらのミスで注文品の納品が遅れたため、弊社に大きな損害が発生したことをお伝えいたします。

貴社の納品が遅れた分だけ、弊社の新事務所の立ち上げも遅れてしまいました。社内で本件について十分に検討を重ねたうえでもう一度ご連絡いたします。最悪の場合、損害賠償を請求する可能性もございます。

よろしくお願いします
山本翔太

Subject: Re: Order for 20 computers

Dear Mr. Brown,

I regret to inform you that our company suffered a serious loss because of your failure to deliver our order on time.

Due to this delay, the launch of our new office was pushed back. We will be in touch with you again once we have carefully considered the matter internally. In the worst-case scenario, we may need you to compensate us for damages.

Kind regards,
Shota Yamamoto

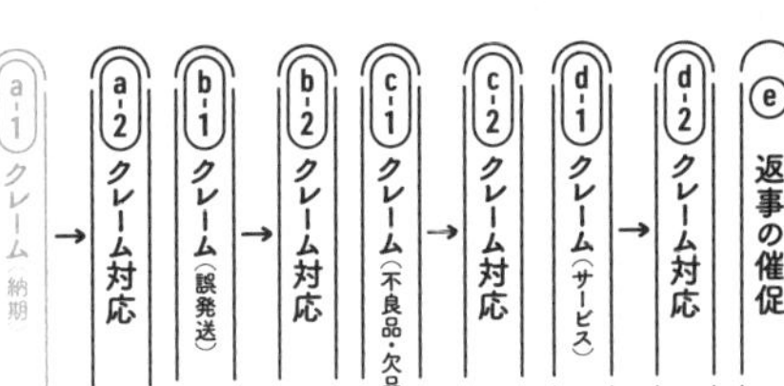

言い換えセンテンス

先日注文した商品がまだ届きません。

My order from a few days ago still hasn't arrived.

注文番号 12345 の品物が、5 月 10 日の時点でまだ到着しておりません。

As of May 10, order 12345 still hasn't arrived.

5 日に到着予定だった商品が、1 週間遅れて届きました。

The product which was supposed to arrive on the 5th came one week late.

至急確認をしていただけますか？

Could you please confirm as soon as possible?

到着予定はいつ頃か再度お知らせいただけますか？

Could you please let me know again when it's supposed to arrive?

ご担当者の方のお名前をいただけますか？

Could you please send us the name of the person in charge?

クライアントも納品を待っております。

The client is also waiting for the delivery.

弊社はこの件を非常に深刻に受けとめています。

We consider this to be a very serious issue.

もう少し、なんとか早めることはできないでしょうか？

Is there any way that you can move it up even a little?

もしすべての商品を同時に配達することが難しければ、まずは一部の注文だけでも先に送っていただくことはできないでしょうか？

If you're not able to deliver the whole order at once, would it be possible for you to send part of the order in advance?

注文の品が届かないと何も進められません。

We can't start on anything if the order doesn't arrive.

今後は再度このようなことが起こらないよう、必要な対策を講じていただきたく存じます。

We'd like you to take necessary measures to ensure such things do not happen again in the future.

今回このような残念な結果となった経緯を教えていただきたいです。

I'd like you to let us know what led to this unfortunate result.

遅延の原因をお調べいただき、今後このようなことがないようにお願いします。

I would appreciate it if you could look into the reason for the delay and make sure something like this doesn't happen again.

今後遅れそうな場合は事前にご連絡をいただきたいです。

In the future, please contact me in advance if it looks like there will be a delay.

大変残念ですが、注文をキャンセルさせていただきます。

Unfortunately, we have decided to cancel our order.

どのような場合でも20日までしか待てません。それまでには荷物が必要です。

In any case, the longest we can wait is the 20th. We need the shipment to arrive before then.

大至急お電話をください。

Please call me immediately.

a-2 クレーム対応

件名：Re: Re：注文した 20 台のノートパソコンについて

翔太様

まだ注文の品が到着していないと伺い、申し訳なく思っています。現在、出荷部門の責任者がこの問題を調査中です。すぐに具体的な情報をお知らせできればと思います。

あらためて、心よりお詫び申し上げます。

よろしくお願いします。
ノア・ブラウン

Subject: Re: Re: 20 laptops we ordered

Dear Shota,

I'm sorry to hear that your order hasn't arrived yet. The head of our shipping department is looking into this problem now. I hope to be able to get you some concrete information very soon.

Again, please accept my sincere apology.

Regards,
Noah Brown

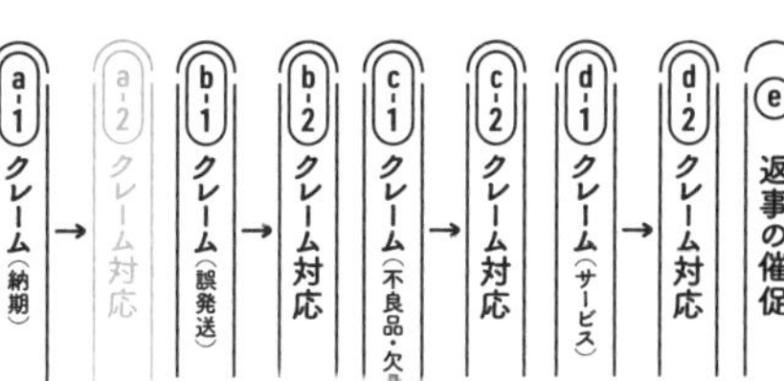

言い換えセンテンス

注文の品がまだ届いていないと聞き、驚いております。

I'm surprised to hear that your order has not arrived yet.

納期の遅れについてのご連絡ありがとうございます。

Thank you for contacting me regarding the delay in the delivery date.

原因を至急確認して、あらためてご連絡いたします。

I will look into the cause right away and contact you again.

この状況をすでに調査しており、すぐに折り返し連絡させていただきます。

We're already looking into this situation, and we'll get back to you soon.

注文の品がいつ確実に届くかを確認いたします。

We'll find out exactly when the order will arrive.

確認したところ、通関に関する書類に不備があったことが分かりました。

After looking into it, we discovered that the customs paperwork wasn't filled out properly.

商品の注文を予想以上にいただいたため、通常より配送に時間がかかっております。

We have received more orders than we expected, so delivery is taking longer than usual.

当社の配送担当が納期を間違えていたことが判明しました。

We found out that the person in charge of delivery on this side got the delivery date wrong.

配送会社の方で配達が遅れているようです。

It looks like there are delays on the delivery company's end.

配送会社に確認したところ、貴社へ配送済みになっているようです。

After checking with the delivery company, it appears that delivery to your company was made.

今一度ご確認いただけませんでしょうか？

Could you check that again for me?

確認したところ、本日到着するようです。

After checking, it looks like it will arrive today.

至急確認し、お手元に届くように手配いたします。

I will check immediately and make sure it arrives.

ご迷惑をおかけして大変申し訳ございません。

I'm terribly sorry for all the trouble.

こちらの手違いで配送が遅れてしまい大変申し訳ございませんでした。

I'm terribly sorry for the delay in delivery our mistake caused.

その間にもし商品が届きましたら、お知らせいただけますか？

In the meantime, could you let me know if it arrives?

納品が遅れましたことをあらためてお詫び申し上げます。

I apologize again for the delay in delivery.

この件を最優先事項とします。

We'll give top priority to this.

b-1 クレーム（誤発送）

件名：【大至急】注文番号 12345 に関して

リンダ様

注文番号 12345 の商品を受け取りましたが、私が注文した内容とは違うものでした。注文の品を大至急送っていただけますでしょうか？ 5月 10 日までにはこちらへ到着するようにお願いいたします。

このメールをご覧になったら、すぐに返信をください。

よろしくお願いいたします。
山本翔太

Subject: Urgent-Regarding order 12345

Dear Linda,

I received order 12345, but it wasn't the item that I ordered. Could you send the correct item as soon as possible? Please arrange so that it arrives here by May 10.

Please respond once you've read this email.

Regards,
Shota Yamamoto

言い換えセンテンス

5月5日に注文した品を受け取りました。

I received the item I ordered on May 5.

お送りいただいた品物に関してお伺いいたします。

I'd like to ask about the item you sent.

注文の品を受け取ってすぐに検品しました。

We inspected the item right after receiving our order.

残念ながら、こちらの注文した製品ではありませんでした。

Unfortunately, we found that it wasn't the item we ordered.

注文とは製品の色が違っていました。

The item is not the color we ordered.

こちらは黒色の品を注文したのですが、中に入っていたのは白色でした。

We ordered a black one, but this one is white.

弊社が注文していない部品100個が送られてきたようです。

It looks like you sent us 100 parts that we did not order.

注文より 100 個多く部品が送られてきたようです。

It looks like you sent us 100 more parts than we ordered.

受け取った品物は、弊社が注文したものではありませんでした。

The items we received were not what we ordered.

添付の写真を参照してください。

Please refer to the attached photos.

弊社はほかの方が注文した品を受け取ったようです。

It looks like we received someone else's order.

見本の色とだいぶ違うようです。

The actual color is quite different from the one in the sample.

遅くとも 9 月 20 日までに商品が必要です。

We need the item by September 20 at the latest.

手違いで受け取った製品をどうすればよいかお知らせください。

Please let us know what we should do with the item we received by mistake.

今後このようなことはないようにお願いいたします。

Please make sure this doesn't happen again in the future.

なぜこのようなことになったのか原因究明をお願いいたします。

Please investigate why this happened.

急いでいるので、いつ頃手配ができるかお知らせください。

I'm in a hurry, so please let me know approximately when you'll be able to send it.

迅速なご対応をお願いいたします。

Your prompt attention is appreciated.

b-2 クレーム対応

件名：Re：【大至急】注文番号 12345 に関して

山本様

注文とは違う製品が届いたというメールを受け取りました。大変失礼いたしました。正しい品を至急発送いたします。

本日発送いたしますので、金曜日までには貴社へ着く予定です。ご迷惑をおかけして大変申し訳ございません。

よろしくお願いします。
リンダ

Subject: re: Urgent-Regarding order 12345

Dear Mr. Yamamoto,

I received your message regarding your incorrect order. I am terribly sorry. I will send the correct item immediately.

I will send it by the end of the day, so the item should arrive at your company by Friday. I'm terribly sorry for all the trouble.

Regards,
Linda

言い換えセンテンス

弊社のミスにより誤発送をしてしまい申し訳ありません。

We apologize for the dispatch error caused by our company's mistake.

現在、大至急発送の準備をしております。

We are currently preparing the shipment to be sent immediately.

商品の到着予定日が分かりましたら、ご連絡いたします。

We will contact you once we know the estimated arrival date of the item.

大変お手数ですが、間違って送ってしまったものをご返送いただけますでしょうか？

I apologize for the inconvenience, but could you please return the item you received by mistake?

間違って届いた品は弊社スタッフが回収しにお伺いいたします。

Our staff will come pick up the item we sent by mistake.

よろしければ間違って送ってしまったものもお使いいただけたらと思います。

If you wish, you're free to use the item we mistakenly sent you.

弊社のミスで、間違った宛先に配送されてしまったようです。

It seems like the item was sent to the wrong address due to a mistake on our company's part.

商品がすぐにお手元に届くように手配いたします。

We will arrange for the item to arrive as soon as possible.

原因を至急確認して、あらためてご連絡させていただきます。

We will look into the cause of the problem immediately and contact you again.

このようなことが二度と起こらないように、すでに措置を講じております。

We have already taken action to ensure that this problem does not occur again.

お詫びに次回のご注文の送料を無料にします。

By way of apology, the shipping on your next order will be free.

この件によって生じた多大なご不便をお詫び申し上げます。

I would like to apologize for the considerable inconvenience this has caused.

現在この件は調査中で、それが済み次第、報告書をお送りいたします。

We are investigating this problem, and we will send you a report of our findings once we have completed the investigation.

お手数をおかけしてしまい誠に申し訳ありません。

We are terribly sorry for the inconvenience we have caused.

製品は5月20日に到着予定です。

The item is set to arrive on May 20.

ご不便をお詫び申し上げるとともに、弊社は再発を防止するために措置を講じております。

We apologize for this inconvenience, and we have taken action to prevent it from happening again.

今後さらなるサービス向上に努めます。

We will work towards improving the quality of our service in the future.

変わらぬお取引をお願い申し上げます。

I hope that our relationship will remain unchanged.

c-1 クレーム（不良品・欠品）

件名：Re：注文した 20 個の時計について

ブラウン様

昨日、注文した品を受け取りましたが、残念ながら 20 個の時計のうち、5 つに欠陥があります。

契約にのっとって、直ちに交換品を送っていただく必要があります。ご連絡お待ちしております。

お願いします
井上大介

Subject: Re: Order for 20 clocks

Dear Mr. Brown,

We received our order yesterday. However, I'm afraid that five of the 20 clocks are defective.

According to the contract, we need you to send replacements right away. I look forward to hearing back from you.

Kind regards,
Daisuke Inoue

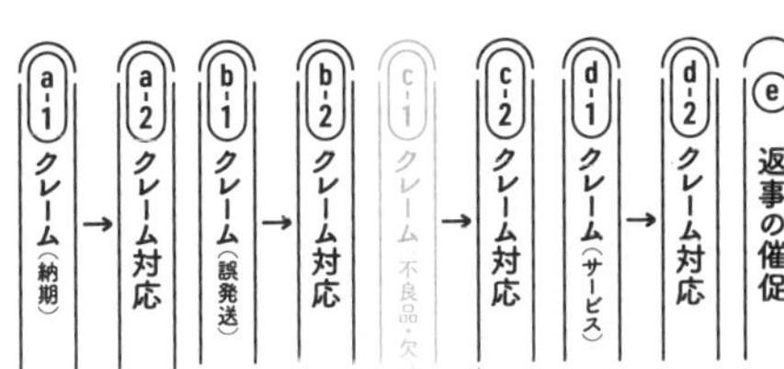

言い換えセンテンス

12345 番の請求書の件です。

This is in regards to invoice No. 12345.

お送りいただいた商品のいくつかにひび割れが確認されました。

Cracks were found in some of the items you sent.

製品番号 1234 を検品しましたが、どれも作動しません。

We inspected item 1234 and found that the unit does not turn on.

製品のほとんどが起動しません。

Most of the items do not turn on.

商品のほとんどが壊れています。

Most of the items have been damaged.

型番 12345 の製品を 100 個注文しましたが、90 個しかありませんでした。

I ordered 100 of product No. 12345, but only 90 have arrived.

残念ながら、部品の 15 個が破損していたのがわかりました。添付写真を参照してください。

Unfortunately, we found that 15 of the parts were damaged. Please refer to the attached photos.

恐れ入りますが、部品が 25 個足りません。

I'm afraid that we are missing 25 parts.

弊社の検品によりサンプルより品質が劣っていることが判明しました。

Our inspection showed that the quality of the items we received are inferior to the sample.

添付の写真の通り、ひどく損傷しています。

They are badly damaged, as shown in the attached photos.

原因を究明いただき、なるべく早く交換品を送っていただけたらと思います。

We'd appreciate it if you could look into this and send us replacements as soon as possible.

すぐに返品したいのですが、返送費用はご負担いただけますか？

I would like to send the items back as soon as possible, but would you be able to cover the return fees?

至急交換品の発送をお願いいたします。

Please send the replacements as soon as possible.

20 日までに弊社の得意先に納品できるように、交換品をお送りください。

Please send the replacements so that we can deliver them to our customer by the 20th.

契約通り、直ちに交換品を送っていただく必要があります。

According to the contract, we need you to send replacements right away.

10日の正午までに確実に荷物が届くように、必要な手配をお願いいたします。

Please do whatever is necessary to make sure the shipment gets here before 12:00 on the 10th.

お電話をお待ちしています。

We'll be waiting for your call.

大至急状況を確認して、ご連絡をお願いいたします。

Please confirm the situation and contact me as soon as you can.

c-2 クレーム対応

件名：Re：注文した 20 個の時計について

井上様

ご迷惑をおかけして大変申し訳ございませんでした。早急に確認をいたしまして、営業部の田中マリから本日中にご連絡をいたします。

ご迷惑をおかけしてしまい、申し訳ございませんでした。ご寛容に感謝いたします。

お客様相談窓口
クリス・ブラウン

Subject: Re: Order for 20 clocks

Dear Mr. Inoue,

We're very sorry for the inconvenience. We'll look into this immediately and have Mari Tanaka in the Sales Department contact you by the end of the day.

Please accept my apology for the inconvenience we have caused you. Thanks for your patience.

Chris Brown
Customer Service Representative

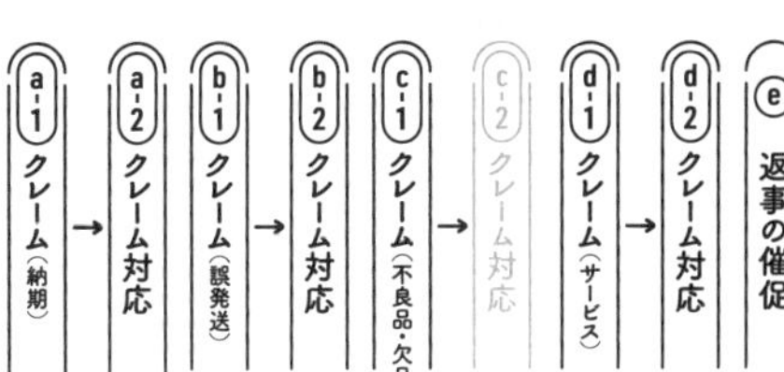

言い換えセンテンス

この件についてお詫び申し上げます。

We would like to apologize for this issue.

欠陥品についてお知らせくださり、ありがとうございます。

Thank you for letting us know about the defective parts.

すぐに担当の者に知らせ、折り返しお電話させるようにいたします。

I'll contact the person in charge and have them call you back.

交換品を 5 個お送りさせていただきました。

We've sent you five replacement items.

発送した品の数が間違っていたとのこと大変失礼いたしました。

I'm very sorry for sending you the wrong number of units.

すぐに不足分を送らせていただきます。

We will send you the missing parts immediately.

現在この件の原因を調査中です。

We are currently investigating the cause of this issue.

この件によって生じた多大なご不便をお詫び申し上げます。

I would like to apologize for the considerable inconvenience this has caused.

ご不便をおわび申し上げるとともに、弊社は再発を防止するために措置を講じております。

We apologize for this inconvenience, and we have taken action to prevent it from happening again.

経緯についてご説明したいのですが、今週お会いすることはできますでしょうか?

I'd like to explain to you what happened. Do you have time to meet with me this week?

原因を調査しておりますので、分かり次第ご連絡いたします。

We are investigating this issue now, and we'll contact you as soon as we know what happened.

交換の品は間もなく到着します。

The replacement will arrive shortly.

ご迷惑をおかけしてしまい、本当に申し訳ございません。

We are sincerely sorry for the inconvenience.

これからも何卒よろしくお願いいたします。

Thank you for your cooperation.

ほかにも何か不具合や気になる点がございましたら、いつでもお知らせください。

If you have any other problems or concerns, please contact us anytime.

今後更なる品質管理の向上に努めさせていただきます。

We will make changes and do a better job with quality control in the future.

あらためて申し訳ありませんでした。

Again, please accept our sincerest apologies.

d-1 クレーム（サービス）

件名：オンライン講座の障害について

こんにちは。

今朝からオンライン講座につながらず、サイト内にそれに関する情報が見当たりませんでした。

復帰のめどがいつ頃か教えてください。

お返事お待ちしています。

ありがとうございます。
高木マサル

Subject: Online course site down

Hello,

I have been unable to access the course site since this morning, and I couldn't find any information about this on your site.

Could you please let me know by when you expect the website to be back online?

I look forward to hearing from you.

Thanks,
Masaru Takagi

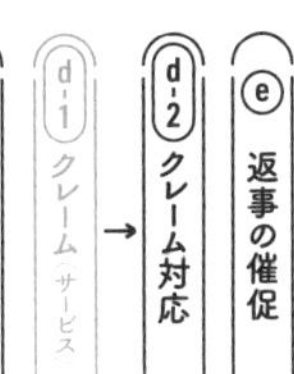

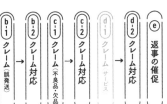

言い換えセンテンス

何度も試していますが、エラーのメッセージが出てしまいます。

I have tried several times, but I keep getting an error message.

サービスが利用できなかった分は返金してもらえますか？

Could I get a refund for the time I was unable to use the service?

今回のトラブルの埋め合わせの割引はありますか？

Will there be a discount to compensate for these issues?

トラブルの原因はなんでしょうか？

What is the reason for this problem?

今朝からログインができません。

I have been unable to log in since this morning.

トラブルが解決したら教えてください。

Please let me know when this problem has been resolved.

全社員が利用しているため、とても困っています。
All of our employees use it, so this is a major problem.

オンライン決済サービスが利用できません。
The online payment service isn't working.

原因を究明して、ただちに復旧をお願いします。
Please figure out the cause of the problem and fix it ASAP.

サービス内容が価格に見合っていないと思います。
I don't think your services are worth the price.

サービスの質がよくありません。
The quality of your service isn't good.

サービスの質がどんどん落ちていると思います。
It seems like the quality of your service is getting worse and worse.

このままの状況であれば、契約を解除せざるを得ません。
I will have to cancel my contract with you if this situation continues.

またこのようなことがあれば貴社のサービスの利用をやめさせていただきます。
I will no longer use your company's services if this happens again.

サービスの向上に努めてください。

Please work on improving your services.

d-2 クレーム対応

件名：Re：オンラインの障害について

マサル様

オンライン講座の件でご迷惑をおかけして大変申し訳ありません。弊社のサーバーがダウンしていたことが原因でした。本日2時から再度ご利用いただける予定です。

この度はご不便をおかけして申し訳ありませんでした。

カスタマー・サービス
カレン・ドノバン

Subject: Re: Online course site down

Hello Masaru,

We are terribly sorry for the trouble regarding our course site. The issue was caused by our servers experiencing an outage. The system should be up and running again by 2:00 p.m.

We apologize for the inconvenience.

Karen Donovan
Customer Service

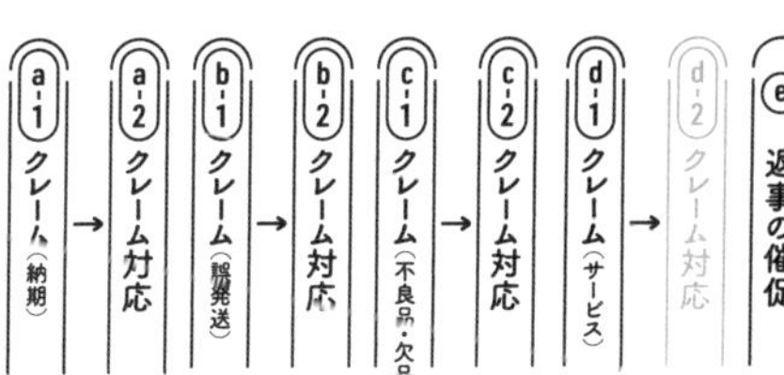

言い換えセンテンス

本日は終日利用いただけません。

The service will be down all day.

原因を早急に調べてご連絡いたします。

We will look into the cause of the issue immediately and contact you soon.

現在原因は不明で、各所に連絡して解決に向けて動いています。

The cause of the problem is currently not known, but we contact with the departments involved and are working to resolve it.

ご不便をおかけして大変申し訳ございません。

We are terribly sorry for the inconvenience.

スタッフの対応の質が悪かったことをお詫びします。

We would like to apologize for the poor service you received from a member of our staff.

今後もサービスの質の向上に努めてまいります。

We will continue to work to improve the quality of our services.

利用できなかった分の料金はいただきません。

You will not have to pay for the time that you were unable to use our services.

来月分の利用料金を無料とさせていただきます。

You may use our services free of charge next month.

開発部部長の田中が事情のご説明とお詫びに貴社に伺います。

Tanaka-san, the head of the Development Department, would like to visit you to explain the situation and apologize.

今後社員教育を徹底いたします。

We will improve our employee training.

大変恐縮ではございますが、原因解明につきましては少しお時間をください。

I'm afraid we still need a little more time to find the cause of the problem.

今後このようなご迷惑をおかけしないために、原因が判明し次第、情報共有を徹底いたします。

To avoid inconvenient events like this in the future, we will be sure to share the cause of the problem as soon as we identify it.

全社をあげて再発防止に努めてまいります。

The entire company will work to ensure this does not happen again.

この度は、誠に申し訳ございませんでした。

We offer our sincere apologies.

至急ご連絡をさせて頂きます。

We will contact you as soon as possible.

いただいたご意見を踏まえ、担当者を厳重に注意いたしました。

We have received your complaint about the individual responsible and have disciplined him accordingly.

弊社の副社長の佐藤からも、本日 3 時までにご連絡させていただきます。

Sato-san, our Vice President, will contact you again by 3:00 today.

(e) 返事の催促

件名：（再送）8月6日の打ち合わせについて

ジョージ様、マイケル様

打ち合わせに関する以下のメールを8月6日にお送りしましたが、まだお返事をいただいていません。

スケジュールを確定させたいので、本日4時までにお返事いただけますか？

お返事をお待ちしております。
山本翔太

Subject: August 6 meeting (resent)

Dear George and Michael,

I haven't received a reply to the email I sent on August 6 regarding our meeting yet.

Could you answer by 4:00 today so I can confirm my schedule?

Hope to hear from you soon,
Shota Yamamoto

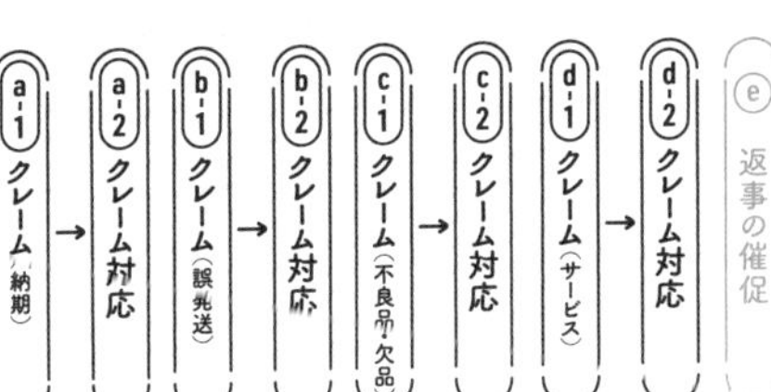

言い換えセンテンス

お送りした請求書へのお返事をまだいただいておりません。

I haven't received a reply to the invoice I sent yet.

弊社のサーバーが原因で届いていないかもしれないと思い、連絡いたしました。

It's possible that it hasn't arrived due to an issue with our company's servers, so I'm contacting you just in case.

下記のメールはお読みいただけましたでしょうか？

I was wondering if you have had a chance to look at the email below.

弊社のメールの不具合でしたら申し訳ありません。

I apologize if it was an issue with our company's email.

大至急お返事をお願いいたします。

I need to ask you to give us an answer as soon as possible.

今日中にお電話をいただけますか？

Could you please call me sometime today?

期日まであと3日しかありません。

There are only three days left before the deadline.

メールでの返信が難しければ、私の携帯（080-122-3344）までご連絡ください。

If it's difficult for you to reply by email, could you call my cell phone (080-122-3344)?

ご連絡心よりお待ちしております。

I look forward to hearing from you.

今週中にお返事をお願いします。

Please answer by the end of this week.

連絡の取りやすいお時間帯はございますか？

Is there a convenient time for me to contact you?

お忙しいとは思いますが、ご対応いただけると助かります。

I know you must be busy, but I would appreciate it if you could respond.

急かして申し訳ございませんが、ご一報ください。

I apologize for rushing you, but please let me know.

とても重要な件ですので、お返事いただけると助かります。

This is a very important matter, so we would appreciate it if you could reply.

この件に関してお返事をいただけると幸いです。

I would be grateful if you could let us have your answer concerning this matter.

何か問題がございましたら、お知らせくださいませ。

Please let us know if there are any problems.

ご協力に感謝します。

Thank you for your cooperation.

このメールをご覧になったらすぐにご連絡をください。

Please contact me immediately once you've read this email.

PART 1
社外とのやりとり

CHAPTER 12
お知らせ

- ⓐ お礼のメール
- ⓑ 訃報
- ⓒ お悔やみ
- ⓓ 励ましなど お見舞い・
- e-1 退職・異動など → e-2 返信（退職・異動など）
- ⓕ 着任のあいさつ・後任の紹介

ⓐ お礼のメール

件名：出張中はお世話になりました

ダニエル様

先週のスイス本社への出張中は大変お世話になりました。

ダニエルさんをはじめ、会社の方々によくしていただきとても助かりました。直接お会いできてうれしかったです。また様々なビジネスの可能性を確認できました。

これからもどうぞよろしくお願いいたします。

村田ミユキ

Subject: Thank you for your help during my visit

Hi Daniel,

Thank you very much for helping me during my trip to the Swiss headquarters last week.

You and everyone at the company were so kind and helpful. I was also glad to be able to meet you in person and to see the many potential business opportunities.

I look forward to working with you in the future.

Miyuki Murata

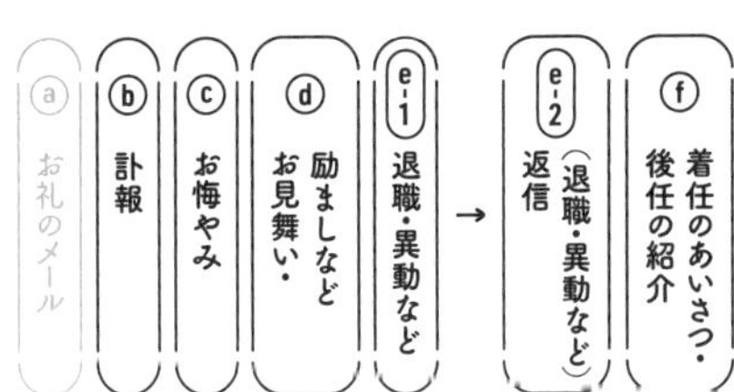

言い換えセンテンス

先週はお世話になりました。
Thank you for helping me last week.

先日はごちそうになり、ありがとうございました。
Thank you for dinner the other day.

滞在中は色々なところへ案内していただき、本当にありがとうございました。
Thank you for showing me around so many places during my visit.

有意義なお話がたくさんできて大満足です。
I'm glad we could have some valuable discussions.

出産祝いを送っていただき誠にありがとうございます。
Thank you very much for the baby gift.

とてもすてきなお祝いの品を頂戴し、感激しております。
Thank you for the lovely gift.

皆様の温かい歓迎に大変感激いたしました。
I truly appreciate the kind welcome.

中村を温かく迎え入れていただきありがとうございます。
Thank you for welcoming Nakamura-san too.

おいしいお料理をありがとうございました。
Thank you for the delicious food.

すてきなレストランを用意してくださり、ありがとうございました。
Thank you for choosing such a lovely restaurant.

お忙しい中いろいろ手配をしていただき、心よりお礼を申し上げます。
Thank you for making all the arrangements at this busy time.

大切に使わせていただきます。
I'll take good care of it.

次回は私にごちそうさせてください。
Next time it's on me.

ぜひ、東京へもいらしてください。
Please come to Tokyo someday.

今度日本へいらしたときはご案内させていただいます。
I'll show you around if you come to Japan.

また近いうちにお会いできることを祈っております。
I hope we can meet again soon.

スタッフの皆様にもよろしくお伝えください。

Please say hello to all the staff too.

ご厚意に感謝しております。

I'm so grateful for your kindness.

ⓑ 訃報

件名：代表の訃報のお知らせ

リンダ様

大変悲しいお知らせがあります。長い闘病の末、弊社代表の山崎カズオが 3 月 10 日に永眠いたしました。

最期のお別れをしたい方のために葬儀を行います。詳細は下記の通りです。

日時：3 月 14 日（金）13：00 ～
場所：聖パウロ教会

ご不明点があれば遠慮なく私宛にメールをください。

よろしくお願いします。
田中ヒロユキ

Subject: News of our president's passing

Dear Linda,

I have some terribly sad news. Our company president, Kazuo Yamazaki, passed away on March 10 after a long illness.

We will be holding a funeral for all those who would like to pay their respects. The details are listed below.

Date: March 14 (Fri) 13:00
Location: St. Paul's Church

Don't hesitate to contact me if anything is unclear.

Sincerely,
Hiroyuki Tanaka

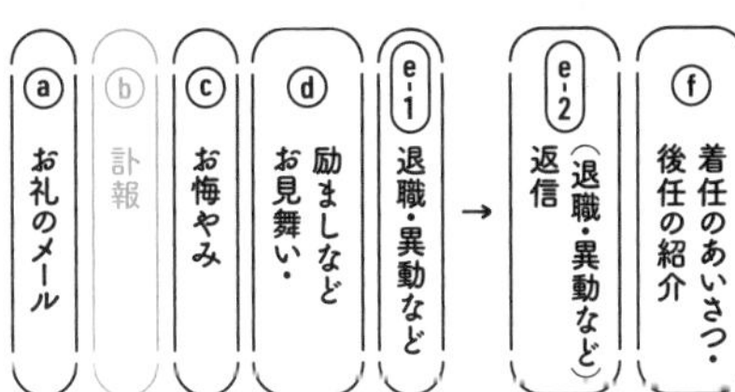

言い換えセンテンス

営業部の伊藤ナオユキさんのお父様が昨日お亡くなりになられたことをお知らせします。

I am sorry to inform you that the father of Naoyuki Ito from the Sales Department passed away yesterday.

山田二郎さんが4月10日に事故に遭われて急逝したとの連絡がありました。

I received the news that Jiro Yamada passed away suddenly after he was involved in an accident on April 10.

ABCインターナショナルのホワイト氏が、昨夜亡くなられたとの連絡がありました。

I received the news that Mr. White from ABC International passed away last night.

葬儀は添付の通り執り行われます。

We will be holding the funeral service as described in the attachment.

葬儀はご家族の方だけで執り行われます。

The funeral will be just for family members.

社葬が執り行われる予定です。

A company funeral will be held.

密葬の儀は近親者にて相済ませました。

A private funeral was held with just close acquaintances.

告別式は社葬の後に、執り行います。

A farewell service will be held after the company funeral.

弊社からは供花を送る予定です。

We plan to send flowers from our company.

弊社からは、社長と副社長が代表で葬儀に出席される予定です。

Our president and vice president will represent our company at the funeral.

葬儀の出席をご希望の方は総務部までご連絡をください。

Those wishing to attend the funeral should contact the General Affairs Department.

葬儀の詳細は追ってお知らせいたします。

We will contact you again at a later date regarding the details of the funeral.

お香典につきましては辞退されるとのことです。

Monetary gifts will not be accepted.

ご家族から、お花や香典は受け取らないとのお申し出がございました。

The family has stated that they will not be accepting flowers or monetary gifts.

葬儀については追ってお知らせいたします。

I'll let you know about the funeral service later.

詳細につきましては追ってご連絡いたします。

We will contact you regarding the details at a later date.

突然のことで社員一同悲しみに暮れております。

All of our staff are saddened by the sudden news.

Ⓒ お悔やみ

件名：お悔やみ申し上げます

ヒロユキ様

貴社の社長マーサ・ピーターセン氏が先週ご逝去されたと伺い、お悔やみ申し上げます。ご遺族様、そして貴社の皆様に哀悼の意を表します。

リンダ

Subject: Deepest sympathies

Dear Hiroyuki,

We were sorry to learn that the president of your company, Ms. Martha Peterson, passed away last week. Please kindly convey our condolences to her family and to everyone in your company.

Linda

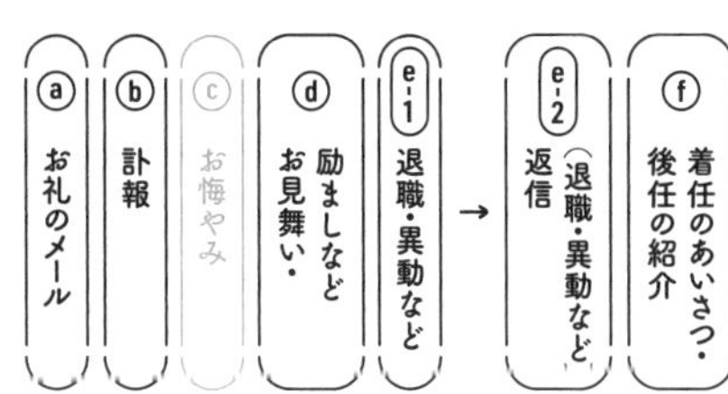

言い換えセンテンス

貴社の社長が亡くなられたとのこと、大変残念に思います。

The passing of your president was very unfortunate.

お父様がご逝去されましたこと、お悔やみ申し上げます。

I was very saddened to hear about the passing of your father.

お母様のご逝去に際し、心よりのお悔やみを申し上げます。

My sincere condolences to you on the passing of your mother.

弊社を代表して、謹んで哀悼の意を捧げます。

On behalf of our entire company, please accept our deepest sympathies.

この度のご不幸に、ご心情を察し胸が痛みます。

My heart goes out to you during this time of sorrow.

お父様のご逝去の報に接し、お悔やみ申し上げます。ABC 社一同、心から哀悼の意を表します。

I was sorry to learn of the passing of your father. Please know that all of us at ABC offer our heartfelt sympathies.

ご家族の皆様に謹んでお悔やみ申し上げます。

We just wanted to let you know that our thoughts are with you and your family.

お父様の思い出とともに悲しみを乗り越えられますように。

May loving memories of you and your father help you find peace.

彼と働く機会を持てたことが誇らしいです。

We feel honored to have had the opportunity to work with him.

故人とともに過ごした日々が偲ばれます。

Someone so special can never be forgotten.

故人には生前、大変にお世話になりました。

He / She helped me in many ways in the past.

私に何かできることがあれば、何でもおっしゃってください。

If there is anything I can do, please let me know.

ご遺族ならびにABC社の皆様に、心よりお悔やみ申し上げます。

Please convey our sincerest condolences to his family and everyone at ABC.

素晴らしい人柄の彼女にもう会えないことを、皆寂しく思っています。

She was truly a great person and we will all miss her.

お悔やみ申し上げます。
Please accept my heartfelt condolences.

ご冥福をお祈りします。
May she/he rest in peace.

力になります。
We are here for you.

私の思いと祈りは、あなたとともにあります。
My thoughts and prayers are with you.

ⓓ お見舞い・励ましなど

ブラウン様

私ども ABC 社はあなたがご入院されていると伺いました。お見舞い申し上げます。1日も早いご復帰を弊社一同願っておりますが、ゆっくり休息されることも願っております。

では。
翔太

Dear Mr. Brown,

Everyone here at ABC was sorry to learn that you are in the hospital. We all hope to see you back at work soon, but we also hope you have a well-deserved rest.

Sincerely yours,
Shota

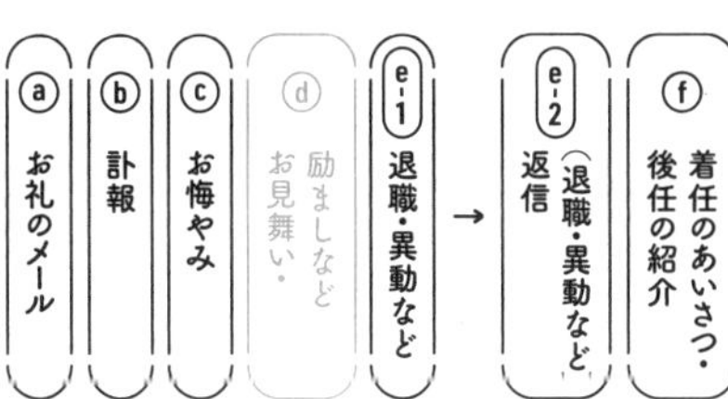

言い換えセンテンス

怪我をされたと伺いました。お見舞い申し上げます。

I'm sorry to hear about your injury.

ご実家が地震の被害に遭われたそうですね。

I heard that your family home was damaged in the earthquake.

社長の１日も早いご全快をお祈りいたします。

We will be praying for a speedy and complete recovery for your president.

お父様の早いご快復を祈っております。

We're hoping for your father's quick recovery.

足の骨を折ったと伺いましたが大丈夫ですか？

I heard that you broke your leg. How are you doing?

具合が悪いと聞いて大変心配しています。

We were so sorry to hear you've been unwell.

可愛がっていたハナちゃんが亡くなったと聞きました、家族の一員を亡くすのはつらいですよね。

I'm sorry to hear of the passing of your beloved Hana. I know it can be painful to lose a member of the family.

皆さん無事ですか？

Is everyone there safe?

何かできることはありますか？

Is there anything I can do to help?

大きな被害に遭われていないことを祈っております。

I hope that the damage is not too serious.

よくなるように願っております。

You are in our thoughts as you get back on your feet.

寂しいから早く回復してね！

Get better soon because we really miss you!

十分にご静養ください。

I hope you will take it easy and take care of yourself.

1日も早い快復を心よりお祈り申し上げます。

I sincerely hope that you make a quick recovery.

1日も早い退院を願っております。

I hope that your stay in the hospital will be brief.

快復後にお目にかかれるのを楽しみにしております。

We're looking forward to seeing you after your recovery.

どうか快復にご専念ください。

Please try to focus on getting better.

元気を出してくださいね。

Please hang in there and get better soon.

e-1 退職・異動など

件名：企画部への異動

ジョンソン様

4月1日付で販売部から企画部へ異動になりましたことをお知らせいたします。

鈴木ユウタが私の後を引き継ぎます。彼はとても優秀で、貴社のお力添えのためにベストを尽くすはずです。

よろしくお願いします
山崎ケイタ

Subject: Transfer to Planning Department

Dear Mr. Johnson,

I'd like to let you know that as of April 1, I will be transferring from the Sales Department to the Planning Department.

Yuta Suzuki will be taking over my responsibilities. I'm sure that you will find that he is very talented and will do everything he can to support you.

Regards,
Keita Yamazaki

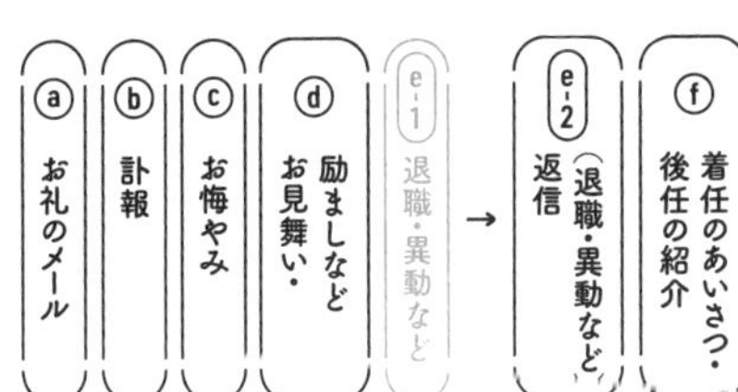

言い換えセンテンス

初めまして。

Hi everyone!

ご報告が遅くなりましたが、今月より名古屋支社で勤務しております。

I'm sorry for the late notice, but since this month I have been working at the Nagoya branch office.

東京支店からこちらに異動してきました。

I just arrived here from the Tokyo branch.

この度、営業部部長へ就任いたしました鈴木太郎です。

I'm Taro Suzuki and I was recently assigned to be the sales manager.

産休に入られたケリーさんより、権利関係の仕事を引き継ぎました。

Kelly is on maternity leave, so I will be taking over the work concerning rights.

ABC 社にて 10 年間楽しく働いて参りましたが、3 月 30 日をもって退職する運びとなりました。

I have enjoyed working at ABC company for 10 years, but I will be resigning on March 30.

何か質問がございましたら、後任の山本翔太までお問い合わせいただけましたら幸いです。

If you have any questions, I would appreciate it if you could contact my successor, Shota Yamamoto.

私は5月25日付でABCを退社し、家業を継ぐことになりましたことをお知らせいたします。

I'd like to let you know that I will be resigning from ABC on May 25 in order to take over my family's business.

地方の小さい企業ではありますが、最善を尽くす所存です。

Although it is a small regional company, I intend to do my very best.

とても去りがたいのですが、ついにその時が来てしまいました。

It's very difficult for me to leave, but the time has come.

お知り合いになれることを楽しみにしています。

I look forward to getting to know each of you.

色々とお教えいただくことになると思いますが、どうぞよろしくお願いします。

I'm sure there is a great deal I can learn from you.

これから一緒に頑張っていきましょう。

Let's do our best going forward.

この仕事に慣れるまで時間がかかると思いますが、ご理解の程どうぞよろしくお願いいたします。

It will take me a while to get used to this job, so I'll need to ask for your understanding.

長年にわたり皆様から賜りましたご厚情に心より感謝いたします。

Thank you very much for the kindness shown to me over the years.

今までありがとうございました。

Thank you for your kindness over the years.

ABC 社で皆様と一緒に働いたことは、とてもいい思い出です。

I have many good memories of the time we spent working together at ABC.

また一緒にお仕事ができることを願っております。

I hope that we will have the opportunity to work together again.

狭い世の中ですので、またどこかでみなさんに再会できることを楽しみにしております。

It's a small world, so I look forward to a time when our paths cross again.

皆様に非常にお世話になったことを忘れません。

I'll never forget everything you've done for me.

e-2 返信（退職・異動など）

件名：お知らせありがとうございます。

リチャード様

部署異動のお知らせありがとうございます。そしておめでとうございます！ 3年間お引立ていただきありがとうございました。今後の更なるご活躍期待しております。

将来また一緒に働ける機会を楽しみにしています。

頑張ってください！
田中マコト

Subject: Thank you for the notification

Dear Richard,

Thank you for letting me know that you will be moving to another department, and congratulations! I appreciate all your help over the last three years, and I'm looking forward to hearing about your continued success.

I hope that we have the opportunity to work together again in the future.

All the best!
Makoto Tanaka

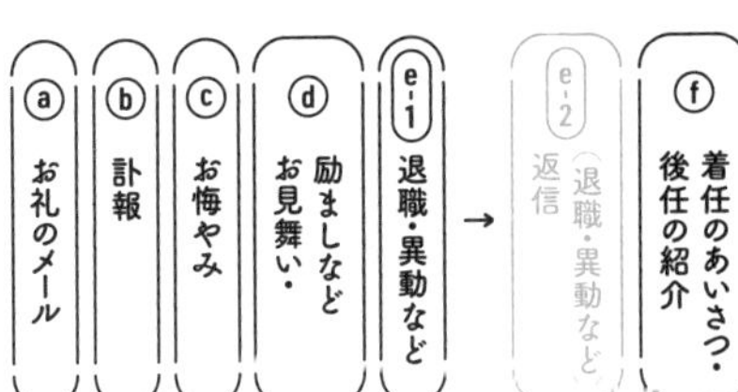

言い換えセンテンス

ご丁寧に異動のご連絡いただきまして、誠にありがとうございました。

Thank you for your kind letter letting me know about your move.

転勤おめでとうございます。

Congratulations on your transfer.

あなたのご尽力に大変感謝しております。

I am very grateful for all your efforts.

転勤、誠におめでとうございます！

Congratulations on your new position!

ロンドン支社へ転勤されるとのご連絡をいただきました。

I got your email announcing your relocation to the London branch.

転勤されると聞き、大変驚いています。

I was very surprised to hear that you had been transferred.

新しい挑戦を楽しみにされていることでしょう。

I'm sure this will be an exciting challenge for you.

お仕事をご一緒できて、とても幸運でした。

I feel very fortunate to have had the opportunity to work with you.

健康に気をつけて引き続き大いに活躍されることと思います。

Please take care of your health, and I wish you the best of luck in the future.

新しい部署で、ますますご活躍されることをお祈りしています。

I'm looking forward to seeing your continued success in the new department.

おかげ様でたくさんのことを学んだ日々でした。

I learned a lot from working with you.

落ち着いたら連絡をしてください。またランチにでも行きましょう。

Please contact me when you get settled in. Let's have lunch together sometime.

またご一緒する機会があるかと思いますので、そのときはどうぞよろしくお願いいたします。

I look forward to having the chance to work with you again.

連絡を取り合いましょう。

Let's keep in touch.

新しい場所でも頑張ってください。

Best wishes for your new position.

こちらへ来る時はぜひお立ち寄りください。

If you have an opportunity to come back, please drop in and see us.

今後どちら様宛てに連絡したらよいか決まったら教えてください。

Please let me know who to contact once it has been decided.

ご成功とご多幸をお祈りしています。

Best wishes for your success and happiness.

ⓕ 着任のあいさつ・後任の紹介

件名：ごあいさつ

ウォルター様

前任の田村から引き継ぎまして、４月から貴社を担当させていいただくこととなりました。

貴社の期待にお応えできるよう、全力を尽くさせていただきます。近いうちに貴社へごあいさつに伺います。

よろしくお願いします
鈴木真衣

Subject: Greetings

Hello Walter,

I'd like to let you know that I have been chosen to succeed Mr. Tamura, and I will have the privilege of being in charge of your account from April.

I will do my best to meet your high expectations and to continue to provide the service you expect from us. I would like to visit your office to introduce myself in person soon.

Sincerely,
Mai Suzuki

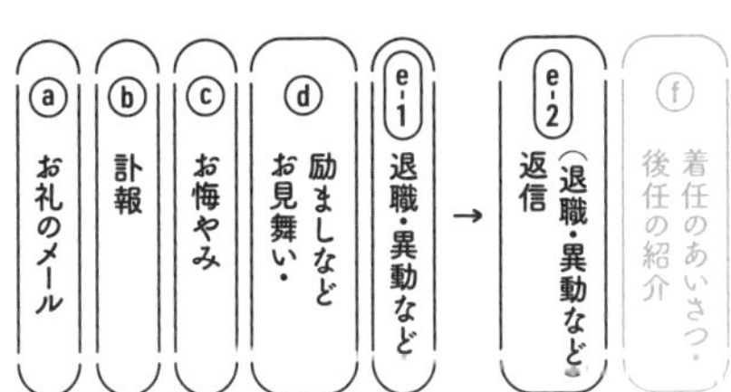

言い換えセンテンス

弊社の田村太郎より連絡があったと思いますが、後任の鈴木真衣と申します。

I believe Taro Tamura from our company has already contacted you, but I am Mai Suzuki, his successor.

来月より NY 支社へ転勤することになりましたのでお知らせいたします。

I'd like to let you know that I will be transferring to the New York branch next month.

次の月から鈴木麻衣が私の仕事を引き継ぎます。

Mai Suzuki will be taking my place from next month.

4 月 1 日付で企画部へ転勤となりました。

I have moved to the Planning Department as of April 1.

先月退職した村田博の後任です。

I'm replacing Hiroshi Murata, who left the company last month.

同僚である山本翔太へ仕事を引き継ぎます。

My co-worker Shota Yamamoto will take over my position.

鈴木真衣が私の後任となります。

Mai Suzuki will take over from me.

新しいアシスタントとして鈴木麻衣が村田太郎のポジションを引き継ぎます。

Mai Suzuki is going to take over Taro Murata's position as your new assistant.

村田太郎に代わってこのプロジェクトを引き継ぎました。

I will maintain this project on behalf of Taro Murata.

先日村田が退職したため、私が貴社の窓口となります。

Taro Murata left us last month, so I will be your new contact.

貴社を担当することができ、大変光栄です。

It is a great honor to be chosen to do business with your company.

貴社とお仕事ができてとても光栄でした。またご一緒できるのを楽しみにしております。

It was great working with you, and I hope to have the opportunity to do so again in the future.

お仕事でご一緒できるのを楽しみにしております。

I look forward to doing business with you.

慣れるまで至らぬ点があるかもしれませんが、その際は遠慮なくご指摘ください。

It will take me some time to get used to this position, so please don't hesitate to give me feedback at any time.

近いうちにごあいさつに伺います。

I will visit you in the near future to introduce myself.

近いうちにお会いできれば幸いです。

I look forward to seeing you in the near future.

弊社の製品について分からないことがあればいつでも連絡ください。

Please contact me if anything is unclear about our products.

数週間は鈴木タケオのサポートを行います。

I'll be supporting Takeo Suzuki for a few weeks.

PART 2
社内のやりとり

CHAPTER 13
報告・質問

ⓐ 報告を求める

→ b-2 質問に答える

ⓐ 報告を求める

件名：売上報告のお願い

マイケルへ

3月～6月までのうちの会社の売上報告をまとめてください。金曜日の会議で使うので明日までにもらえると助かります。

忙しいところすみませんが、お願いします。

よろしく。
山田稔

Subject: Request for sales report

Dear Michael,

Please compile a report on our company's sales from March to June. I want to use it in Friday's meeting, so I would appreciate it if you could send it to me by tomorrow.

Thank you for taking time out of your busy schedule to do this.

Best,
Minoru Yamada

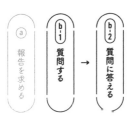

言い換えセンテンス

キャンペーンの成果を報告してください。

Please report the results of the campaign.

プロジェクトの状況を把握したいので進捗を知らせてください。

I want to understand the situation surrounding the project, so please let me know how it's going.

直近 5 年分の売上報告書を送ってください。

Please make a report of sales from the last five years.

中間報告をしてください。

Please give an interim report.

次の会議で売上の中間報告をお願いします。

Please make an interim report at the next meeting.

月毎の売上高を報告してください。

Please make a month-by-month sales report.

プロジェクトの進捗状況を報告してください。

Please report on the progress of the project.

今起きている問題点を報告してください。

Please report on any problems you are currently facing.

チーム内の問題点を突きとめて、次の会議で報告してください。

Please identify the problems facing the team and report them at the next meeting.

自分なりに問題点を探って報告書にまとめてください。

Please identify any problems you see happening and sum them up in a report.

改善案を話し合って結果を報告してください。

Please discuss an improvement plan and report the results.

急ぎではないので手が空いたときにお願いします。

It's not urgent, so you can do it whenever you have some free time.

できるだけ早くメールで送ってください。

Please send it by email as soon as possible.

いつ頃に報告できそうか教えてください。

Please let me know when you will be able to make the report.

忙しい時期に申し訳ないけど、大切なことなのでお願いします。

I know this is a busy time for you, but it's important.

売上報告から分かったことをみんなでシェアして、今後に生かしたいと思います。

I want to share the findings of the sales report with everyone and utilize them in the future.

部長が正確な売上数字を知りたいそうです。

The department head wants an accurate sales figure.

ざっくりした数字で構いません。

A rough estimate is fine.

b-1 質問する

件名：金曜日の会議についての質問です

エレンへ

会議で何を話し合うか知っていますか？ 昨日は外出していたので何も聞いていません。

手が空いたときに教えてもらえると助かります。

お願いします。
麻衣

Subject: A question about Friday's meeting

Hi Ellen,

Do you know what will be discussed at the meeting? I was out all day yesterday, so I haven't heard anything.

I would appreciate it if you could give me a rundown when you get some free time.

Best,
Mai

言い換えセンテンス

提出してくれた企画書について質問があります。
I have a question about this business proposal you submitted.

会議の参加人数は分かりますか？
Do you know how many people will be at the meeting?

会議の場所はどこか分かりますか？
Do you know where the meeting will be held?

このプロジェクトの担当者が誰か分かりますか？
Do you know who's in charge of this project?

製品の発売日については誰に聞いたらいいですか？
Who should I ask about the release date of the product?

会議で話したプロモーションは進んでいますか？
How is the promotion we talked about at the meeting going?

報告書で分からない箇所があります。
There's something I'm not sure of in the report.

報告書の数字は何を基にしたものですか？

What did you base the numbers in the report on?

DEF 社の担当者は誰ですか？

Who's in charge of communicating with DEF?

お手間かけます。

Thanks in advance.

なるべく早めに返事をください。

Please reply as soon as you can.

返事は急ぎません。

There's no rush.

何か分からない点があれば遠慮なくお知らせください。

Don't hesitate to let me know if something is unclear.

分からなければ、誰に聞けばいいか教えてください。

If you're unsure, please let me know who else I could ask.

b-2 質問に答える

件名 : Re : 金曜日の会議についての質問

麻衣へ

昨日質問のあった会議の内容についてですが、メインの議題は以下の通りです。
・来年の広告キャンペーンについて
・来月からのチーム編成について

会議は 3 月 15 日第 7 会議室にて 11 時～の予定です。他にも不明点があればお知らせ下さいね。

よろしく
エレン

Subject: Re: A question about Friday's meeting

Hi Mai,

Regarding the meeting agenda you asked about yesterday, these are the main topics:
- Next year's new advertising campaign
- The makeup of the teams from next month

The meeting will be in Room 7 from 11:00 on March 15. Please let me know if anything else is unclear.

Best,
Ellen

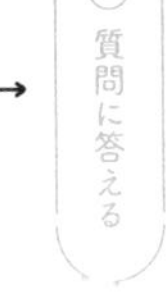

言い換えセンテンス

このプロジェクトの担当者は企画部の鈴木さんです。

Mr. Suzuki from the Planning Department is in charge of this project.

報告書は、経理部の売上報告書を参考に作成しました。

I based my report on the Accounting Department's sales report.

DEF 社の担当は山本さんだと思います。

I think Mr. Yamamoto is in charge of relations with DEF.

DEF 社の担当は確か山本さんだと思いますが念の為確認します。

I think Mr. Yamamoto is the one in charge of relations with DEF, but I'll double-check just in case.

進捗状況ですが、クライアントの承認待ちです。

Regarding the progress of the project, I'm waiting for approval from the client.

進捗の報告が遅れてすみません。添付の通り順調です。

I'm sorry for reporting the progress late. You'll see by looking through the attachments that it's going well.

すぐに確認して折り返しメールします。

I'll double-check immediately and get back to you.

報告書の数字は、販売部の田中さんに借りた資料を基にしています。

The numbers in the report are based on the materials I borrowed from Mr. Tanaka from the Sales Department.

この報告書を作成したのは私ではないので分かりません。

I'm not the one who produced this report, so I'm not sure.

申し訳ないのですが分かりません。

I'm sorry, but I don't know.

マイクが担当なので直接聞いてください。

Mike is in charge of that, so please ask him directly.

担当のマイクに確認いたしますので少しお待ちください。

Mike is the one in charge of that, so please wait a moment while I ask him.

調べるのに少し時間ください。

Please give me some time to look it up.

分からないので分かり次第メールします。

I don't know yet, but I'll message you when I figure it out.

分かりそうな人に聞いてみますね。

I'll ask someone who probably knows.

CHAPTER 14

アイデアや意見の募集

ⓐ チームに向けて

ⓑ 社内投票

ⓐ チームに向けて

件名：キャンペーンサイトへのアイデア募集

チームの皆さんへ

キャンペーンサイトへのアイデアの募集をします。次回のDEF社との会議に向けて、各自企画書を作成してください。会議の前日の1月27日までに私宛てに送ってください。

忙しいとは思いますが、本プロジェクトには社運がかかっています。

よろしくお願いいたします。
ダニエル・ウルフ

Subject: Looking for ideas for the campaign website

Hello team members,

I'm looking for some ideas for the campaign website. I'd like to ask everyone to make a proposal individually in preparation for the meeting with DEF. Please send them to me by January 27, the day before the meeting.

I know you all are busy, but this is a very important project for the future of the company.

Thanks in advance
Daniel Wolf

言い換えセンテンス

DEF社との共同プロジェクトに向けて、提案があればお知らせください。

Let me know if you have any ideas regarding our joint project with DEF.

ざっくりした内容でいいのでお知らせください。

All ideas are welcome. They don't have to be specific.

チームの効率を向上させるためのアイデアを募集します。

I'm looking for ideas to improve team efficiency.

売上増につながるような提案を皆さんから伺いたいです。

Please let me know if anyone has any ideas to increase profits.

この機会にぜひ自分の考えを発表してください。

Please use this opportunity to share your thoughts with everyone.

具体的な運営方法も併せて提示してください。

Please also submit ideas for concrete management methods.

必要なコストも考慮して提案してください。

Please also think about the estimated cost of your project.

まずは気軽にアイデアを募りたいと思います。

To get started, please send me anything that comes to mind.

この件について皆さんの意見を聞きたいので、金曜日に会議を開こうと思います。

I'd like to hold a meeting on Friday to hear everyone's ideas about this.

5月10日午後2時から、新しい支店に関するブレインストーミングを行いたいと思います。

I want to hold a brainstorming session about our new branch store on May 10 from 2:00.

このプロジェクトにおける改善案を提案してください。

Please send any ideas you may have about how to improve the project.

収益化するには何をしたらいいか各自考えてください。

Please individually think about how we can make this profitable.

事業化および商品化につながるような現実的なアイデアを募集しています。

I'm looking for realistic ideas to create a new project or product.

積極的にご提案ください。

Don't hesitate to send your proposals.

各自今週中に考えをまとめておいてください。

Please individually prepare your ideas by the end of this week.

どんなに単純な提案でも夢に近いものでもいいので、あらゆるアイデアをお待ちしています。

You can send me any and all ideas no matter how mundane or unrealistic they are.

あなたのアイデアを実現できるチャンスかもしれません。

This may be a chance to turn your idea into reality.

誰かと共同でアイデアを提案しても OK です。

You can propose an idea together with someone else.

ⓑ 社内投票

件名：社内投票

社員の皆様へ

会社のマスコットキャラクターの名称を投票で決定したいと思います。以下の内どれがいいかを明記して、メールで投票してください。

A：ピカりん
B：マッシュくん
C：ユメミル

回答期日は9月30日の午後12時までです。投票お待ちしております。

企画開発部
山口マナミ

Subject: Company vote

Hello everyone,

I'd like to hold a vote to decide the name of the company's mascot. Please reply to this email and indicate which of the names below you like.

A. Pikarin
B. Mr. Mush
C. Yumemiru

The due date for responses is 12:00 p.m., September 30. I look forward to receiving your votes.

Manami Yamaguchi
Planning and Development Department

言い換えセンテンス

時代の流れを考慮して、弊社も時間差通勤の導入を検討しています。

To keep up with the times, our company is also considering allowing flexible working hours.

フレックスタイムの導入について検討しています。賛成か否かをメールにて投票してください。

We are considering allowing flexible working hours. Please email me stating whether you agree or disagree.

自動販売機の撤去についてのアンケートにご協力ください。

Please fill out this survey regarding the removal of vending machines from the company.

リモートワークを導入するかどうか投票で決めることになりました。

We have decided to hold a vote to determine whether we will start teleworking or not.

賛成・反対の意見は全て検討させていただきますので、下記のアンケートにご協力ください。

We will consider all assenting or dissenting opinions, so please fill out the survey below.

投票結果を会社の移転先の候補地の参考にはしますが、決定するものではありません。

The results of the vote will only be used to gather ideas for the company's new location, so the decision is not set in stone.

これはウォーターサーバーかコーヒーマシンのどちらを設置したいかのアンケートです。

This is a survey regarding whether we want a water cooler or coffee machine.

新製品の第一印象についてのアンケートを実施することになりました。

We decided to conduct a survey regarding first impressions of the new product.

ご協力いただける方にはサンプルを配布します。

We will distribute samples to everyone who participates.

添付したデザインのうち、どれが一番 40 代の女性に受け入れられるでしょうか？

Out of the attached designs, which do you think women in their 40s would like the most?

下記 URL の投票画面にてご投票ください。

Please send your votes through the website below.

全社員の皆様に、ご協力いただく必要があります。

We need all staff to participate.

今週の金曜日に回答を締め切ります。

Responses are due by Friday.

投票結果は一斉メールにてお知らせします。

We will send the results of the vote out to everyone by email.

必ず期日内にお返事ください。

Please make sure to respond by the deadline.

期日を過ぎての投票は無効となります。

Votes submitted after the deadline will not be accepted.

アンケートの締め切りは5月20日（木）です。メールで回答をお願いします。

The deadline for the survey is May 20 (Thu). Please respond by email.

アンケートは任意ですが、なるべくお答えください。

The survey is optional, but please participate if possible.

CHAPTER 15 作業のヘルプを頼む

1-a 作業のヘルプを頼む①
1-b 作業のヘルプを頼む②
1-c 作業のヘルプを頼む③
→
2-a 対応する①
2-b 対応する②
③ リマインド

1-a 作業のヘルプを頼む①

件名：仕事のお願い

エイミーへ

販売部の小森ミノルです。１つ頼みたいことがあってメールしました。以下のメールを海外に出したいので、英語にしてもらいたいです。丁寧な英語でお願いします。

忙しいところすみませんが、よろしくお願いします。

どうもありがとう。
小森ミノル

Subject: Could you help me out?

Hi Amy,

I'm Minoru Komori from Sales, and I'd like to ask you for some help. I have to send an email overseas, but it needs to be in English. Could I ask you to translate it into polite English?

I know you must be busy, but I'd appreciate your assistance.

Many thanks,
Minoru Komori

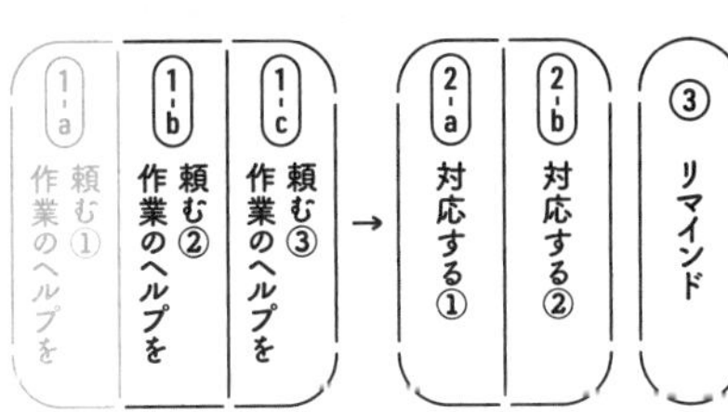

言い換えセンテンス

1つ至急のお願いがあります。

I have an urgent request.

企画書を見て意見をもらえますか？

Could you look at the proposal and give us your input?

資料作成の手伝いをお願いしてもいいですか？

I'd like to ask you to help me prepare the materials.

私の代わりに DEF 社に書類を送ってもらえますか？

Could you send the documents to DEF for me?

クライアントへの提案書に問題がないか確認してもらえますか？

Could you check and make sure the proposal to the client looks okay?

DEF 社のクラウンさんを紹介してもらえますか？

Could you introduce me to Mr. Crown from DEF?

DEF 社のクラウンさんの連絡先を教えてもらえますか？

Could you give me the contact information for Mr. Crown from DEF?

どちらのデザインがいいか意見を聞かせてもらえますか?

Could you give us your thoughts on which design is better?

WEB デザインでお勧めの会社があったら教えてください。

If you have any recommendations for a web design company, please let us know.

翻訳が上手な方がいたら推薦してもらえますか?

Could you recommend someone who is good at translating?

お時間なければ結構です。

If you don't have time, it's no problem.

もし時間があったらとても助かります。

If you have time, it would be a big help.

よろしければ詳細を電話または、お会いして説明いたします。

If you have time, I'd like to call you or meet you in person to explain the details.

今週のどこかで 1 時間ほどお時間いただければ十分です。

If you could give me an hour this week, that should be enough.

ご不明な点があればいつでも手を貸します。

If you have any questions, I'd be happy to help at any time.

他部署の仕事をお願いしてしまってすみません。

I'm sorry for making you work in a different department.

ありがとう！ 近いうちにランチをごちそうします。

Thanks! I'll treat you to lunch one of these days.

借りは必ず返します。

I'll return the favor!

忙しいところ申し訳ないけど、引き受けてもらえると助かります。

I know you're busy, but it would be great if you could help us.

1-b 作業のヘルプを頼む②

件名：資料作成のお願い

麻衣へ

自社の売上とXYZ社の売上が比較できる表を作成してメールで送ってもらえますか？ 金曜日までに欲しいです。

忙しいところ申し訳ないけどお願いします。

よろしくお願いします。
テイラー

Subject: Request for materials

Dear Mai,

Could you please prepare a graph comparing our earnings with XYZ's and email it to me? I need it by Friday.

I know you're busy, so thanks in advance.

Best,
Taylor

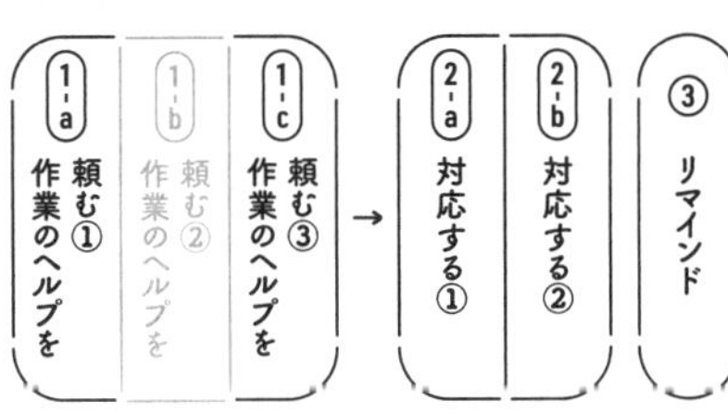

言い換えセンテンス

会議資料の作成を今すぐにお願いします。

Could you prepare some materials for the meeting right away?

私の代わりに打ち合わせに出席していただけますか？

Do you think you could attend the meeting in my place?

急用ができたので、手伝ってもらえますか？

Something urgent has come up, so could you help me out?

会議室の予約をお願いできますか？

Could I ask you to reserve a meeting room?

明日の会議の資料を 30 部コピーしておいてもらえますか？

Could you make 30 copies of the materials for tomorrow's meeting?

Zoom 会議のリンクを出してもらえますか？

Could you send me the Zoom link?

進捗状況をメールで知らせてもらえますか？

Could you send me a progress report by email?

何が起こっているのか教えていただけたら、とても助かります。

I would really appreciate it if you could tell me what is going on.

先ほどの会議の内容を報告書にまとめておいてもらえますか？

Could you summarize what happened at the meeting in a report?

企画書を2、3個考えて、来週の月曜日までに提出してください。

Could you develop two or three proposals and send them to me by next Monday?

代わりにメールで返事しておいてもらえますか？

Could you reply by email on my behalf?

全ての準備を整えるようにお願いします。

I'd like to ask you to get everything ready.

できれば最優先にやってもらいたいです。

If possible, I'd like you to make this top priority.

完了したらメールで知らせてください。

Please email me when you finish.

大至急手配をお願いします。

Please make arrangements ASAP.

突然の変更ですみません。

I apologize for the sudden change in direction.

面倒なプロジェクトですが、手を貸していただき感謝しています。

I know it's a troublesome project, but I appreciate your help.

頼りにしています。

I'm counting on you.

1-c 作業のヘルプを頼む③

件名：英文チェックのお願い

エイミー様

英文チェックのお願いがあります。以下の英文ですが、間違いがないかチェックをしてください。間違いをすべて直して、修正版を金曜日までに送ってください。

ありがとうございます。
山本翔太

Subject: Request for English check

Hi Amy,

I'd like to ask you to check the English text below. Please correct any mistakes you find and send the corrected version to me by Friday.

Thank you,
Shota Yamamoto

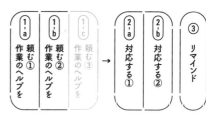

言い換えセンテンス

大至急以下の英文のチェックをお願いします。

Please check the following English text as soon as possible.

添付の英文のチェックをお願いします。

Please check the attached English text.

致命的なミスだけ拾ってください。

Please correct only the major mistakes.

不自然な文章は自然な文章に変えてください。

Please rewrite any unnatural sentences and make them sound natural.

できるだけ丁寧な文章を心がけてください。

Please make it sound as polite as possible.

できるだけ早めにチェックをお願いします。

Please check it as soon as you can.

いつ頃までに終えられそうか教えてください。

Please let me know when you'll be able to finish it.

何か不明点があればお知らせください。
Please let us know if anything is unclear.

スペルチェックはこちらで行います。
I'll check the spelling myself.

不自然な箇所があればどんどん直してください。
Please fix anything you think sounds unnatural.

なるべく元の文章を生かしてください。
Please try to use the original text as much as possible.

表記も統一してください。
Please make sure the expressions are uniform.

大切なクライアントへ提出する書類です。
These documents will be sent to an important client.

誤解がないように、できるだけシンプルな文章にしてください。
Try to keep the text as simple as possible to avoid misunderstandings.

量が多いので、誰かと手分けしていただいてもいいですよ。
There is a lot of text, so, you can share the work with someone else.

急なお願いに対応いただき、ありがとうございます。

Thank you for accepting this on short notice.

終わったら知らせてください。

Please contact me when you finish this.

急ぎではないので、手が空いたときに取りかかってください。

It's not urgent, so start when you have some free time.

2-a 対応する①

件名：Re：仕事のお願い

ミノル様

メールを英語に翻訳する件、もちろん大丈夫です。文章を送ってください。早速、取りかかります。

締め切りがあれば教えてください。

お待ちしています。
エイミー

Subject: Re: Could you help me out?

Hi Minoru,

Of course, I'll be happy to translate the email into English. Please send me the text and I'll do it right away.

If there's a deadline, please let me know.

Waiting to hear from you,
Amy

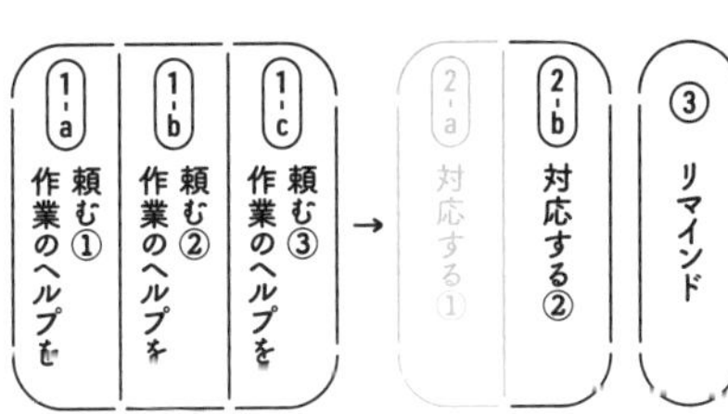

言い換えセンテンス

書類仕事のお手伝い、喜んでやります。

I'll be happy to help you with the paperwork.

詳細をすぐに送ってください。

Please send me the details right away.

できますので、会ってそのことについて話しましょう。

I can do it, so let's meet up and talk about it.

もし急ぎであれば、分担して進められるかもしれません。

If you're in a hurry, maybe we can split up the work.

お受けしたいところですが、私も今とても忙しいのです。

I'd like to accept it, but I'm also very busy right now.

あいにく今週出張なので、引き受けるのは厳しいです。

Unfortunately I will be on a business trip this week, so it will be difficult for me to do.

時間の余裕がないため、残念ながら手伝えないと思います。

I don't have any extra time, so I'm afraid I won't be able to help.

残念ですがその分野には詳しくありません。

I'm afraid I'm not familiar with this field.

締め切りによっては力になれるかもしれません。

I might be able to help, depending on the deadline.

期日をもう少し延ばすことは可能ですか？

Is it possible to extend the deadline a little?

この種の仕事はエリカに手助けを求めた方がいいです。

For this type of work, it's better to ask Erica for help.

手伝えなくて申し訳ありません。

I'm sorry I can't help you.

来週なら手が空きそうなのですが、それでは遅いですか？

It looks like I'll be free next week, if it's not too late.

助けたいところなのですが、今回はお断りしないといけません。

I'd like to help, but I'll have to decline this time.

他にやってくれそうな人がいないか周りに聞いてみます。

I'll see if someone else can handle this.

誰かできる人がいないか探しますね。

I'll look for someone who can do this.

入力のお手伝いなら喜んでします。

I'm happy to help with the input anytime.

他にも何か私に出来ることがあれば遠慮なく言ってください。

Feel free to ask me there's anything else I can do.

2-b 対応する②

件名：Re：資料作成のお願い

テイラーへ

大丈夫です。問題ありません。

金曜日までを目指しますが、遅れる場合は連絡しますね。

よろしくお願いします。
麻衣

Subject: Re: Request for materials

Hi Taylor,

Sure, no problem.

I'll try to finish by Friday, but if there are any delays, I'll let you know.

Best,
Mai

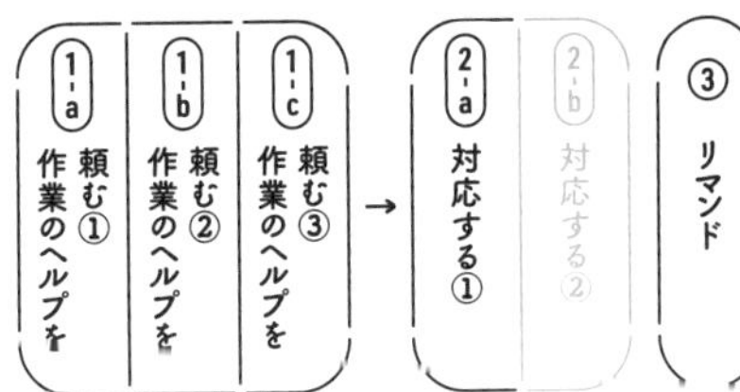

言い換えセンテンス

メールに添付しましたのでご確認ください。

Please see the attachments to this email.

かしこまりました。すぐに準備に取りかかります。

Understood. I'll get started on preparations soon.

もちろん大丈夫です。期日までに仕上げます。

Of course, no problem. I'll get it done by the deadline.

あいにくちょうど今手一杯なので、他の人に頼んでもらえますか？

Unfortunately my hands are full at the moment, so could you please ask someone else?

今忙しいので、締め切りを延ばしてもらえますか？

I'm busy now, so would it be possible to extend the deadline?

今週は時間があるので、できる限り早く取りかかります。

I have some time this week, so I'll get started on it ASAP.

これから外出してしまうので、佐藤さんに頼んでおきます。
I have to go out now, so I'll ask Mr. Sato to do it.

その日は別の約束があるので出席できません。
I have another engagement that day, so I can't attend.

あいにく手元に資料がないので、もう少しお時間いただけますか？
I unfortunately don't have the materials on me, so could you wait just a little longer?

すぐに取りかかりますが、最低３日は時間が欲しいです。
I'll get started on it soon, but I need at least three days.

残念ですが、私は適任ではない気がします。
I'm sorry, but I don't think I'm the best person for this job.

誰かと分担してもいいですか？
Could I work on this together with someone else?

もう少し詳しい内容を聞きたいので後で電話します。
I'd like to clarify the details of the assignment, so I'll call you later.

いつまでにお送りすればいいですか?
When should I send it by?

お受けしたいのはやまやまなのですが、どうしても時間が取れません。
As much as I would like to help, I just can't make time.

お受けできずにすみません。
I'm sorry for not being able to help.

来週はかなり時間があるので、何かあれば声かけてください。
I'm pretty free next week, so please contact me then if you need anything.

他にも何かあれば言ってください。
Please let me know if there's anything else.

③ リマインド

件名：リマインダー：明日締め切りの ABC 社の資料

エイミー様

リマインドのご連絡です。お願いした ABC 社の書類作成ですが、明日が締め切りです。今日もらえたらありがたいのですが、もう少し時間が必要ならお知らせください。

ありがとうございます。
マコト

Subject: Reminder: ABC documents due tomorrow

Hi Amy,

This is just a reminder: The deadline for the ABC documents I asked you to make is tomorrow. It would be great to have them today, but if you need more time let me know.

Thanks,
Makoto

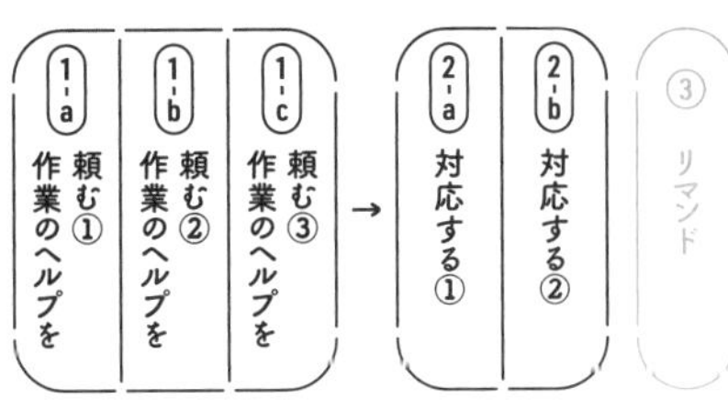

言い換えセンテンス

打ち合わせのリマインドです。

This is a reminder about the meeting.

DEF社との会議は今週金曜日です。

The meeting with DEF is this Friday.

歓迎会の出欠につきましてご予定はいかがでしょう?

Will you be able to attend the welcome party?

打ち合わせの日程が迫ってまいりましたので再度詳細を送ります。

The date of the meeting is approaching, so I am sending the details again.

来週の打ち合わせの内容については、あらためてご連絡いたします。

I'll contact you again regarding the agenda for next week's meeting.

お願いしていたプロジェクトの期限が本日ですが、進捗状況を確認したいと思います。

The deadline for the project I asked you to do is today, so I wanted to check on how things are going.

提出期限を過ぎているのでメールしました。

I'm writing because the deadline has passed.

お願いしていた資料がまだ届いてないので、確認しています。

I haven't received the requested materials yet, so I'm just checking.

何か問題があれば教えてください。

Please let me know if there are any problems.

まだお返事をいただいてないため連絡しました。

I'm trying to contact you because I haven't received a reply yet.

スケジュールをあらためて確認してください。

Please check your schedule again.

すでにお返事をいただいていましたら申し訳ございません。

I apologize if you have already responded to me.

お忙しいと思いますが、お忘れなきように念の為のお知らせでした。

I know you're busy, but this is just a little reminder, just in case you have forgotten.

もう少し時間が必要ならすぐに連絡ください。

Please contact me ASAP if you need a little more time.

参加できない場合は、すぐに連絡をください。

Please contact me immediately if you can't attend.

ご迷惑をおかけして申し訳ありませんが、ご確認いただけますか?

I apologize for the inconvenience, but could you please check on this?

お手数をおかけしますが、お返事よろしくお願いします。

I apologize for the inconvenience, but thank you in advance for your reply.

急かしてしまいすみませんが、いつ完成するか教えてください。

I'm sorry to rush you, but please let me know when it will be finished.

PART 2
社内のやりとり

CHAPTER 16
コミュニケーション

ⓖ 仕事を割り振る

ⓕ 遅れることを伝える会議に

ⓔ 代理出席を頼む会議の

ⓓ なぐさめる

ⓒ 上司への相談・ミスの指摘

ⓑ 苦言を呈する

ⓐ ほめる

ⓐ ほめる

カレンへ

先日は重要なプレゼンお疲れさまでした。

とてもよい出来で、クライアントも関心を持ったようです。

このプロジェクトを任せたいと思います。私も社長もあなたにとても期待しています。

頑張ってくださいね！

よろしく。
ネイト

Karen,

Thank you for your work on the big presentation the other day.

It was very well done and it looks as though the client might be interested.

We would like for you to be in charge of the project. Both myself and the company president expect good things from you.

Please give it your all!

Regards,
Nate

give it your all は try your best もしくは do your best でも可

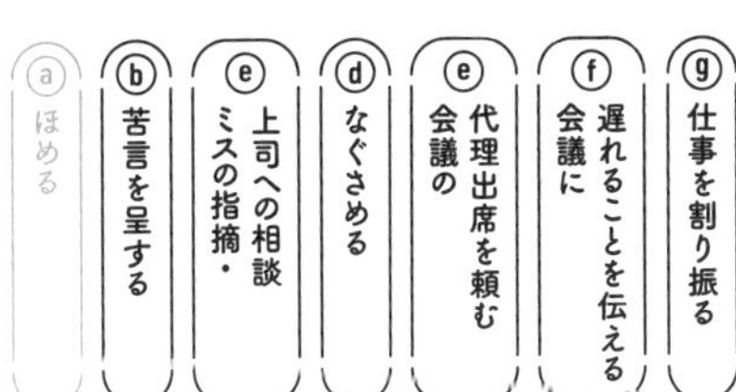

言い換えセンテンス

あなたが毎日遅くまで頑張っていた努力が報われましたね。

The hard work you have put in working late every night has paid off.

部署のみんなもとても喜んでいます。

Everyone in the department is pleased.

提案にはクライアントも満足してくれたようです。

The client was quite pleased with our proposal.

いつも丁寧に資料を作成してくれてありがとう。

Thank you as always for your careful presentation of materials.

今日の報告の内容にはとても感心しました。

Today's report was impressive.

いつも鋭い意見をありがとう。

Thank you for always giving perceptive opinions.

いつも意見を共有してくれてありがとう。

Thank you for always sharing your opinions.

いつもとても具体的な提案をしてくれるのでとても助かります。

Always giving concrete suggestions is a huge help.

あなたの企画のおかげで来週には話が成立しそうです。

Thanks to your planning, we will be able to come to a decision next week.

細かいところも気がついてくれて助かっています。

Thank you for always noticing small details.

すばらしいアイディアで皆を盛り上げてくれていますよね。

You always get everyone excited with your unique ideas.

クライアントからいつもあなたについてのよい点を耳にします。

We always hear good things about you from the client.

よい仕事をするので、任せられる人だとみんな思っています。

We know that we can count on you to do a good job.

いい仕事をし続けて皆によい影響を与えることを願っています。

I hope that you'll continue to do a good job and have a positive influence on everyone.

これからもあなたの頑張りに期待しています。

We look forward to your continued efforts.

このプロジェクトはあなたなら任せられると分かっています。

I know I can count on you to make this project a success.

何か話し合う必要があればいつでも遠慮なく連絡してください。

Please feel free to contact me at any time if you need to discuss anything.

いつでも私を頼ってくださいね。

You can count on me.

あなたの頑張りにみんな感謝していますよ。

Everyone appreciates all of your hard work.

ⓑ 苦言を呈する

件名：納期の遅れについて

トッドへ

クライアントへの納期遅れが続いているようですね。

クライアントと信頼関係を築くことがいちばん大事な仕事です。一度失うと取り戻すのは難しいです。

今後は必ず納期に間に合うようにしてください。

また分からないことがあれば、遠慮なく私に相談してくださいね。

ミシェル

Subject: Regarding late delivery

Dear Todd,

It appears that deliveries to the client continue to be late.

Creating trust with our clients is our number one job and once that trust is broken, it is not easy to regain.

Going forward, be sure to meet delivery deadlines.

Please feel free to contact me if you have any further questions.

Michelle

言い換えセンテンス

最近、欠勤が続いているようですね。
You've missed a lot of work days recently.

連絡をきちんとするのが職場の基本的なルールです。
Clear communication is a basic rule of the workplace.

困ったことがあれば共有してください。
If you are having trouble, please let me know.

仕事があまりに忙しいのであれば、他の人に振り分けて手伝ってもらうなどしてください。
If you feel that you are too busy with work, please try to give some to other staff so that they can help.

クライアントからクレームが来ています。
We've received a complaint from the client.

クライアントからの要望には応えなくてはいけません。
We must abide by the client's wishes.

何か理由があれば教えてください。
If there is a reason, please tell me.

勤務態度を改めるように努力してください。

Please try to improve your attitude towards work.

部署のみんなも困っています。

Everyone in the department is troubled by this.

この事について直接話したいです

I would like to talk with you in person about this.

困ったことがあれば、手助けを頼むようにしてください。

If you're having problems, please be sure to ask your coworkers for help.

状況を改善するために何か私にできることはありますか?

Is there anything I can do to help improve the situation?

周りと協力することはとても大切です。

It's very important to cooperate with each other.

今後改善しない場合は、減給の可能性もあります。

If we don't see an improvement, we may have to reduce your salary.

1人で仕事を抱え込むのはよくありません。

It's not good to take on all of the work by yourself.

もし話したいことがあるなら何でも教えてください。

If there's anything at all that you want to talk about, let me know.

これから精いっぱい頑張ってください。

Please try your best in the future.

あなたからの返答を待っています。

I'm looking forward to your response.

ⓒ ミスの指摘・上司への相談

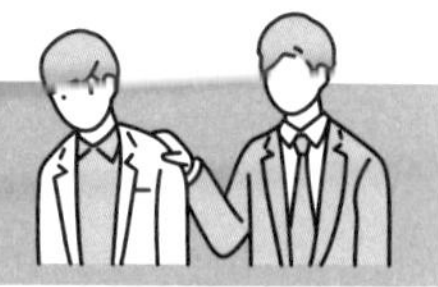

件名：12 月 17 日の鈴木さん宛のメールのミス

マイケルへ

12 月 17 日に ABC 社の鈴木さんへ送ったメールですが、内容に重大な誤りがありました。

私の認識では納期は 12 月 30 日までで 1 月 30 日ではありません。

思い違いだったらすみませんが、ご確認いただけますか？

よろしくお願いします。
翔太

Subject A mistake in the December 17 email to Mr. Suzuki

Hi Michael,

On December 17, an email was sent to Mr. Suzuki from ABC. However, there is one serious mistake in this message.

We agreed that the delivery date would be December 30, not January 30.

I apologize if I have misunderstood anything, but could you please check this?

Thanks,
Shota

ⓐほめる
ⓑ苦言を呈する
ⓒ上司への相談・ミスの指摘
ⓓなぐさめる
ⓔ代理出席を頼む会議の
ⓕ遅れることを伝える会議に
ⓖ仕事を割り振る

言い換えセンテンス

一斉メールにいくつか誤りがありました。

There were some mistakes in the group email.

日付が間違っています。

The date is incorrect.

添付ファイルがありませんでした。

There were no attachments.

ABC 社の担当者は、間違いなく山田さんではなく山口さんです。

I'm quite sure the person in charge at ABC is Yamaguchi-san, not Yamada-san.

送っていただいた資料ですが、いくつか抜けがありました。

There were a few things missing from the materials you sent.

この書類を作成したのは私ではありません。

I'm not the person who wrote this document.

私だけ仕事量が他の人よりも多いように思います。

It seems that I have a heavier workload than anyone else.

ここ数カ月残業しない日がありません。

Over the past few months, there hasn't been a single day when I haven't worked overtime.

ずっと土日も仕事をしているのに、仕事が終わりません。

I work Saturdays and Sundays, but I still don't have time to finish everything.

有給を取りたいのに、取れません。

I want to take a paid vacation day, but I am unable to.

チームのメンバーが協力的ではありません。

The team members are not supportive or helpful.

仕事のプレッシャーに押しつぶされそうです。

I feel like I'm being crushed by all of the pressure from work.

私の勘違いだったら申し訳ございません。

My apologies if I have misunderstood something.

念の為確認させていただきました。

Just to be on the safe side, I have confirmed this information.

我慢が限界を超えそうなので、相談しました。

I am near my breaking point, which is why I am consulting you.

いつもサポートしてもらって感謝しています。

I always appreciate your support.

いつも間に立ってもらってすみません。

I apologize for always putting you in the middle.

わがままを言うようで申し訳ありません。

I apologize if I sound selfish.

ⓓ なぐさめる

件名：この間の発注ミスについて

カレンへ

この間の発注ミスのことだけど、そんなに気にしないように。

人間誰でも間違いはあります。

これから気をつければ問題ありません。

ちょっと気晴らしにお茶にでも行きましょう！

クリス

Subject: Regarding the ordering mistake

Karen,

Try not to worry too much about the ordering mistake the other day.

We're only human and everyone makes mistakes sometimes.

Just make sure to be careful going forward and there won't be any problems.

Let's go out for tea to take our minds off of things for a little while!

Chris

さっきの発注ミス、あまり深く考え過ぎないようにね。

Don't worry too much about the ordering mistake.

あまり落ち込まないでね。

Don't be too upset about it.

慣れるのに時間がかかります。

It'll take some time to get used to things.

私も一度同じミスをしました。

I've made the exact same mistake before.

次から気をつけましょう。

Let's just be careful going forward.

今回の失敗を次に生かしましょう。

Let's learn from this mistake.

プレゼンは失敗に終わったけど、資料はよく出来ていたよ。

The presentation ended in failure, but the materials were well put together.

同じ間違いを繰り返さないことが大事です。

It is important not to repeat the same mistakes.

残念な結果だったけど、あたなにとってよい経験でした。

It didn't turn out the way we had expected, but it was a good experience for you.

私がきちんとフォローするから安心してね。

I'll follow up, so don't worry.

今後もミスを恐れずに挑戦してほしいです。

We'd like you to try again without worrying about making mistakes.

何か悩み事や不安なことがあれば、私に遠慮なく相談して。

If you are ever troubled or worried about anything, don't hesitate to ask me for advice.

最初から完璧にできる人なんていません。

Nobody does anything perfectly the first time.

あなたはやればできるとみんな分かっています。

We all knew you could do it if you tried.

みんなあなたを応援しています。

We're all rooting for you.

おいしいものでも食べに行って元気を出しましょう！

Let's go eat something good to cheer ourselves up!

いつも本当に助かっています。

You're always such a big help.

いつでも力になるので、遠慮なく声をかけてね。

I'm always available to help, so please don't be afraid to ask.

ⓔ 会議の代理出席を頼む

件名：代理をお願いできますか？

ジェシーへ

明日、４時からの営業会議に出席する予定でしたが、急に大切なクライアントから呼び出しがかかりました。

大変申し訳ありませんが、私の代わりに会議に出席していただけますか？

恩に着ます。

翔太

Subject: Could you take over for me?

Hi Jessie,

I was scheduled to attend the sales meeting tomorrow from 4:00, but an important client suddenly asked to meet with me.

I'm terribly sorry, but could you take my place at the meeting?

I owe you one.

Shota

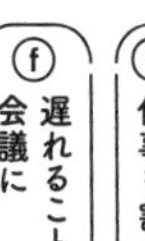

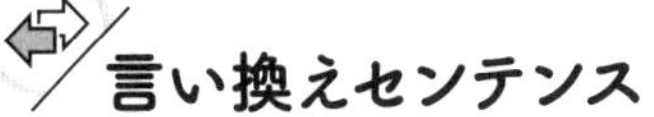

言い換えセンテンス

明日の 4 時に予定されている営業会議があります。

I have a sales meeting scheduled for tomorrow at 4:00.

申し訳ありませんが、急用ができてしまいました。

I'm afraid something urgent has come up.

私の代わりに打ち合わせに出席していただけますか？

Do you think you could attend the meeting in my place?

体調が悪くなってしまったので、代わりに会議に出席してもらえますか？

I'm not feeling well, so could you take my place at the meeting?

あなたならプロジェクトの内容も把握しているので、問題ないと思います。

You understand the contents of the project, so it shouldn't be a problem.

問題が発生してしまい、会議に間に合いそうにありません。

An issue came up, so I don't think I'll be able to make it to the meeting on time.

その日の代理出席が可能かどうか、教えてください。
Please let me know if you will be able to sit in for me on that day.

できるかどうか今日中にお返事ください。
Please let me know by the end of today if you'll be able to do it.

お忙しい中、助けていただきありがとうございます。
I know you must be busy, but I would really appreciate your help.

急なお願いですみません。
I'm sorry for asking you so suddenly.

もしやっていただけるのであれば、詳しい資料を送ります。
If you're able to do it, I'll send you the detailed materials.

もしやっていただけるのであれば、電話ですべて詳しく説明します。
If you're able to do it, I'll call you and explain everything in detail.

ⓕ 会議に遅れることを伝える

件名：明日の会議について

翔太様

明日の午前10時からのXYZ社との打ち合わせですが、遅れてしまいそうです。

顧客のところに寄るので、30分ほど遅れます。先に始めておいてください。

なるべく早く出席できるように努力します。

ご迷惑おかけしてすみません。

ありがとう。
ジェシー

Subject: About tomorrow's meeting

Dear Shota,

It looks like I'll be late to the meeting with XYZ scheduled for 10:00 a.m. tomorrow.

I need to visit a client, so I'll be around 30 minutes late. Please start without me.

I'll do my best to get there as soon as possible.

Sorry for all the trouble.

Thank you,
Jessie

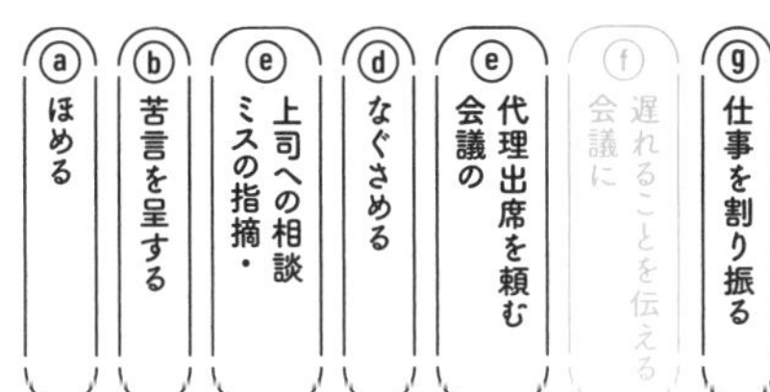

言い換えセンテンス

申し訳ないのですが、明日の会議に少し遅れそうです。

I'm sorry, but it looks like I'll be a little late for tomorrow's meeting.

30 分ほど遅れそうです。

Sorry, I'll be about 30 minutes late.

病院に寄ってから向かいます。

I'll go after I go to the hospital.

母を病院に送ってから出社します。

I'll go into the office after taking my mother to the hospital.

進行役をお任せしてもいいですか？

Could I ask you to be the MC?

MC = master of ceremonies の略で、会議などの仕切り役、司会者のことです。

議事録を取っておいてください。

Please record what happens at the meeting.

すみませんが、電車が止まってしまいました。

Sorry, my train is stopped.

すみませんが今向かっています。

Sorry, I'm on my way.

私のフライトが遅れています。

My flight has been delayed.

悪天候で飛行機が飛ばず、もう1泊することになりそうです。

The plane can't fly due to bad weather, so it looks like I'll have to stay here another night.

お客様に謝っておいてください。

Please apologize to the customer.

他のメンバーにも伝えておいてください。

Please also tell the other members.

私抜きで始めてください。

Please go ahead and start without me.

できるだけ早く行きます。

I'll go as fast as I can.

また連絡して状況を伝えます。

I'll contact you again later about the situation.

場合によっては会議を欠席するかもしれません。

I may not be able to attend the meeting.

何かあれば電話をください。

Please call me if something comes up.

⑨ 仕事を割り振る

件名：生産性向上のための提案

翔太様

現在、私たちの部署は 4 つのグループに分かれています。しかしながら、最近の仕事の進捗状況などを考慮して、1 カ月ほど、2 つのグループで仕事を進めるべきです。

これが生産性を大幅に改善し、納期に間に合うのに役に立つと考えます。

品質管理部
アクセル・ベイカー

Subject: A suggestion to improve productivity

Dear Shota,

As of now, our department is divided into four groups. However, considering the recent progress of our work, perhaps we should try working in two groups for about a month.

This could greatly improve productivity and help us meet deadlines.

Axel Baker
Quality Control Department

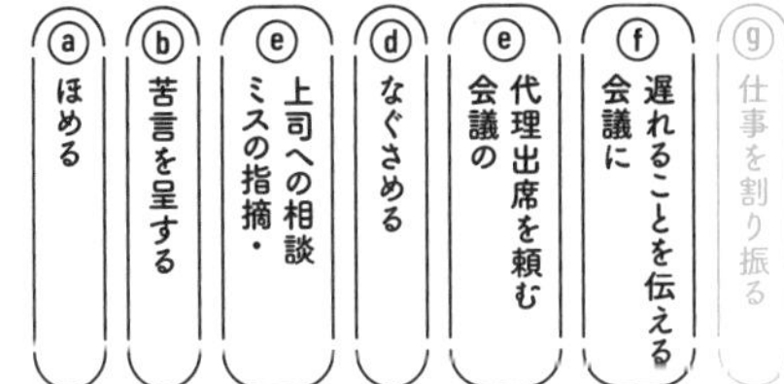

言い換えセンテンス

生産性が向上する提案をしたいと思います。

I'd like to make a suggestion that could improve productivity.

担当の変更を提案します。

I suggest changing the person in charge.

役割を決めたので、添付の作業分担表を確認してください。

I've decided the roles, so please check the attached duty allocation table.

私たちの現在の状況を考慮すると、この変更を行う必要があると思います。

Considering our present situation, I think we need to make this change.

現在、作業効率はあまりよくありません。

Currently, our productivity isn't very good.

現状は１人に負担が偏っています。

Right now, there is too much of a burden on one person.

マイクにチームのリーダーになってもらいます。

I'll appoint Mike team leader.

この決定は皆が能力を最大限発揮するためのものです。

This decision was made so everyone could best use their talents.

この変更によって、締め切りに間に合わせることができるでしょう。

These changes would help us to meet deadlines.

この変更なしに、期日前に終えることは非常に難しいでしょう。

Without these changes, it will be very difficult to meet deadlines.

この変更は来週から実行します。

We will implement these changes from next week.

このチーム編成でしばらく様子を見たいと思います。

Let's see how things go with this team for now.

仕事量が公平になるように調整しました。

I made adjustments to make sure everyone's workload is fair.

異議のある方は返信してください。

Please reply if you have any objections.

変更に困惑している人は直接連絡をください。

Please contact me directly if you are confused about the changes.

他にいい改善案があれば大歓迎です。

Other improvement suggestions are also welcome.

この変更で業務効率が改善することを願っています。

I hope that these changes will improve our work efficiency.

PART 2
社内の人とのやりとり

CHAPTER 17
社内ウェブ会議

社内ウェブ会議

件名：Zoom 会議のお知らせ

企画部の皆様

12 月 10 日に企画部の会議を Zoom で行うことになりました。来春発売の新製品の企画会議になります。11 時になりましたら、以下の URL をクリックして会議にご参加ください。

それまでに各自企画書を提出してください。

ありがとう。
ジェイソン

Subject: Zoom meeting notification

Dear Planning Department members,

The Planning Department will hold a Zoom meeting on December 10. The meeting will deal with our new product which will go on sale next spring. Please click on the link below at 11:00 to join the meeting.

I would like to ask everyone to submit a proposal individually by that time.

Thanks,
Jason

言い換えセンテンス

参加はこちらから：www.zoom.us/0000
Join the meeting: www.zoom.us/0000

オンラインミーティングについてお知らせします。
This is to let you know about the online meeting.

Zoom を使ってオンライン会議を行います。
We will have an online meeting on Zoom.

事前に Zoom のアプリをダウンロードしておいてください。
Please download the Zoom app beforehand.

事前にマイクとカメラのテストを行ったうえでご参加ください。
Please test your microphone and camera before joining.

音声は全員 ON にしたままご参加ください。
Please leave your sound on throughout the meeting.

音声は質問するときだけ ON にしてください。
Please turn on your sound only when asking a question.

カメラは ON にしておいてください。

Please turn on your camera.

リンクをクリックすると Zoom のアプリケーションが立ち上がり、参加できます。

You will be able to join after starting the Zoom app by clicking the link.

会議の 5 分前からつながるようにしておきます。

I will open the meeting five minutes before the start time.

全員に見えるように質問やコメントはチャットで行ってください。

Please send all your questions and comments to the chat so they can be seen by everyone.

カメラを切って参加しても OK です。

You may also participate without using your camera.

会議で共有したい資料があれば事前にご送付ください。

If you have any materials you'd like to share during the meeting, please send them to me beforehand.

会議中に聞こえづらいことがあればチャットでお知らせください。

Please let us know in the chat if you experience any sound problems during the meeting.

スマートフォンでも会議に参加できますが、画面が見えづらいのでPCがお勧めです。

You can join the meeting from a smartphone, but it's hard to see the screen, so we recommend using a computer.

その他、不明な点があれば気軽にご連絡ください。

Don't hesitate to contact me if anything else is unclear.

参加できない場合は早めにご連絡ください。

Please let me know as soon as possible if you cannot attend.

PART 2
社内の人とのやりとり

CHAPTER 18
人事・総務

- ⓐ 社内公募
- ⓑ 会社の業績の報告
- ⓒ リモートワーク導入
- ⓓ 感染症対策／健康管理
- ⓔ ハラスメント対策
- ⓕ 社内イベントの告知
- ⓖ 社内発表
- ⓗ 経費精算・有給休暇

ⓐ 社内公募

件名：新規プロジェクトのメンバー募集

皆様

DEF社との共同プロジェクトに伴い、チームメンバーを増員することになりました。増員にあたり、社内公募を行います。募集要項は添付の通りです。

ご興味ある方の応募をお待ちしております。

企画部
山本翔太

Subject: Looking for new project members

Hi everyone,

We have decided to increase the number of team members working on the joint project with DEF and will be recruiting in-house. The application requirements are as shown in the attachment.

We are looking forward to hearing from interested people.

Shota Yamamoto
Planning Department

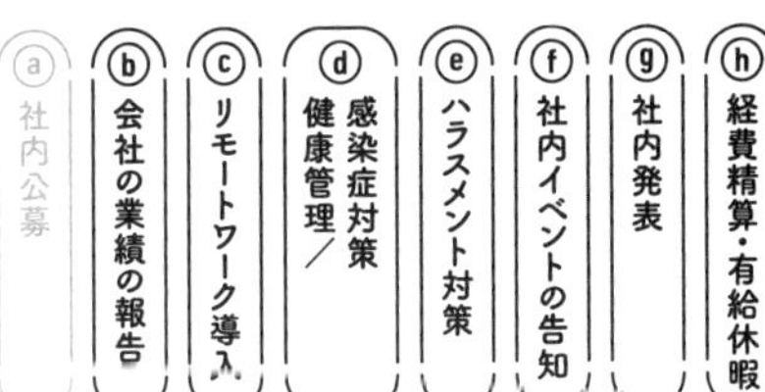

言い換えセンテンス

自社サービスの拡大に伴い、営業チームの統括・指揮をするスタッフを募集します。

We are recruiting staff to supervise and direct the sales team as we expand our services.

新製品の名称を社内公募いたします。

We are asking staff for name suggestions for a new product.

拡大に伴い、国内に支店を増設することになりました。

As we expand, we have decided to add more branches in Japan.

新しい分野への進出に伴い、web ディレクターの募集を行います。

We are looking for a web director to help us enter a new field.

マネージャー職の社内公募を行います。

We are recruiting managers in-house.

能力とやる気のある方を探しています。

We are looking for people who are skilled and motivated.

志望理由を書いて人事部の宮田ジュンコまでご送付ください。

Please write a short essay on why you are interested and send it to Junko Miyata in the Human Resources Department.

選考方法は以下の通りです。

The selection method is as follows:

書類審査後、プロジェクトメンバーとの面談を実施します。

After reviewing the documents, we will ask you to come in for an interview with the project members.

やる気のある人を募集します。

We are looking for motivated people.

応募資格は以下の通りです。

The qualifications for application are as follows:

応募資格や詳細は添付資料をご確認ください。

Please check the attached materials for application qualifications and details.

プロジェクトのリーダー経験 3 年以上必須です。

At least three years of experience as a project leader is required.

WEB デザイン経験者を優遇します。

We prefer those who have experience in web design.

ご興味ある方はぜひご応募ください。

If you have any interest, please feel free to apply.

応募の締め切りは 12 月 20 日となっております。

The application deadline is December 20.

選考日程については追って応募者に連絡します。

Applicants will be notified of the selection schedule.

選考過程の詳細については、企画部の山田さんにお問い合わせください。

For more information about the selection process, please contact Yamada-san in the Planning Department.

ⓑ 会社の業績の報告

件名：4～6月期の売上報告

皆様

4月～6月の売上についてご報告いたします。新製品に関しては当初の目標額の2倍を達成いたしました。詳しくは添付の売上報告書をご確認ください。

この調子で引き続き売上を伸ばしていけたらと思います。

ご協力よ様ろしくお願いいたします。

営業部
田中マナブ

Subject: Sales report for the April-June period

Dear all,

I have an announcement regarding our sales between April and June. We achieved twice our original sales goal with the new product. Please see the attached sales report for details.

Let's keep working to grow our sales even more.

Thank you all for your cooperation.

Manabu Tanaka
Sales Department

言い換えセンテンス

製品に関するクレームを共有します。
I will share the complaints we have received about our products.

出張報告は以下の通りです。
Below is a report on our business trip.

下半期の当社の売上についてご報告いたします。
We would like to report on our sales for the second half of the year.

添付にまとめましたのでご確認ください。
Please check the attached summary.

今年の自社の売上をグラフにまとめたのでご確認ください。
Please check the graph showing this year's sales.

プロジェクトの進捗状況をご報告申し上げます。
We would like to report on the progress of the project.

DEF 社との納品トラブルについてご報告いたします。
We would like to report on the delivery problems with DEF.

目標金額を達成しました。

We have achieved our target.

目標金額には残念ながら届きませんでした。

Unfortunately, the target amount was not reached.

目標額 800 万円に対して達成額は 600 万円にとどまりました。

We achieved only 6 million yen compared to the target amount of 8 million yen.

目標額を大きく上回りました。

We greatly exceeded the target amount.

今後の課題などが見えてきました。

I can foresee some future issues.

皆さんの頑張りのおかげで黒字となりました。

Thanks to everyone's hard work, we made a profit.

今後このようなことが再発しないよう取り組む必要があります。

We need to do our best to prevent this from happening again in the future.

報告の詳細について分からないところがあればお知らせください。

Please let us know if you have any questions about the details of the report.

報告は以上です。

This completes our report.

お手すきの際に、ご確認のほどお願いいたします。

Please check it when you have time.

Ⓒ リモートワーク導入

件名：リモートワーク導入のお知らせ

皆様

この度、感染症対策に伴い弊社でもリモートワークを導入することになりました。期間は２月２日～４月末日までを予定しております。状況により延期もしくは短縮いたします。ご協力お願いいたします。

人事部
鈴木真衣

Subject: Notice regarding implementation of remote work

Hello everyone,

As an infection prevention measure, we have decided to implement remote work. We plan to implement it from February 2 to the end of April. This time period may be shortened or extended depending on the situation. Thanks for your cooperation.

Mai Suzuki
Personnel Department

言い換えセンテンス

リモートワークに関するお知らせです。

This is a notice regarding remote work.

感染の拡大に伴い、リモートワークを実施することになりました。

Due to rising infection numbers, we have decided to implement remote work.

できるだけ自宅で仕事をするようにしてください。

Please do as much work at home as possible.

原則的に出社は週に２日までにしてください。

As a general rule, please come to the office no more than two days per week.

出社日数などは各部署で話し合ってください。

Please discuss in-office days with your department.

感染の収束に伴い、リモートワークを解除することになりました。

Due to improving infection numbers, we have decided to end remote work.

６月１日からリモートワークは解除となります。

Remote work will end effective June 1.

引き続きリモートワークを希望する場合は部長に許可を得てください。
If you would like to continue to work from home, please get approval from your department head.

リモートワークについてルールを設定しました。
We have established some rules regarding remote work.

リモートワークの場合でも勤務時間に変更はありません。
Your work hours will not change, even with remote work.

リモートワークと出社のどちらかを選んでください。
Please choose to work from home or in the office.

リモートワークを選択した場合は、交通費は支払われません。
Those who choose to do remote work will not receive a transportation allowance.

リモートワークの方にはネット通信費として 5,000 円が支給されます。
Those who choose remote work will receive a 5,000-yen internet allowance.

お試しなので、うまくいかない場合はリモートワークを撤廃します。
This is a trial, so if it does not go well, remote work will be cancelled.

コアタイムにはパソコンの前にいるようにしてください。

Please make sure you are at your computer during core time.

会議もできるだけ対面ではなくZoomを利用してください。

Please try to hold meetings over Zoom rather than in-person as much as possible.

やむを得ず出社する場合は管理部に必ず報告してください。

If coming to the office is unavoidable, please inform management.

ⓓ 健康管理／感染症対策

件名：会社によるインフルエンザ予防接種のお知らせ

本年度も会社によるインフルエンザ予防接種を11月3日～5日で1Fのロビーにて行います。総務部に個別にメールで申し込んでください。

医療機関で個別に予防接種を受け、全額自己負担した際は申請により補助金を支給します。

ご不明な点は健康管理課へ直接お問い合わせください。

マリア

Subject: Company influenza vaccinations

The company will be offering flu shots again this year from November 3 to 5 in the 1st floor lobby. Please email the General Affairs Department individually to sign up.

If you receive a vaccination at a medical institution and pay the full amount, you will receive a subsidy upon application.

If you have any questions, please contact the Health Management Division directly.

Maria

言い換えセンテンス

健康診断についてお知らせです。

I would like to inform you about the health checkup.

感染症予防についてのお知らせです。

This is a notice about protection against infectious diseases.

詳細は ABC 健保のウェブサイトを見てください。

For more information, please visit the ABC Health Insurance Society website.

対象はアルバイトや契約社員を含む全社員になります。

The program is open to all employees, including part-time and contract employees.

2 月の末日までに健康診断を受けてください。

Please receive a medical checkup by the end of February.

予約制になります。

Reservations are required.

感染症対策の一環で予約はウェブのみになります。

As part of our infection control measures, appointments can only be made online.

送られてくる注意事項をよく読んでください。

Please carefully read the notes sent to you.

部署でそれぞれ工夫して感染症の対策を行ってください。

Each department should devise its own countermeasures against infectious diseases.

社内での感染を防ぐため、手洗いと換気の徹底をお願いいたします。

In order to prevent infection inside the company, please wash your hands thoroughly and use good ventilation.

部屋をまめに換気してください。

Be sure to ventilate the room frequently.

感染症対策のため、大人数での集まりは控えてください。

To prevent infection, please refrain from gathering in large groups.

席で食事を取るときは私語を慎みましょう。

When eating at your desk, please refrain from chatting.

自費で健康診断を受けた場合は領収証が必要です。

If you receive a medical checkup at your own expense, you need to get a receipt.

業務を円滑に行うためにも健康管理を各自で行ってください。

Please take care of your own health in order to facilitate your work.

規定項目以外の検査については自己負担でお願いします。

For tests other than those specified, please pay on your own.

問診票は直接ご自宅に郵送されます。

The medical questionnaire will be mailed directly to your home.

ご理解とご協力の程よろしくお願いいたします。

Thank you for your understanding and cooperation.

積極的に健康診断を受けてください。

Please be proactive and get a health checkup.

ⓔ ハラスメント対策

件名：ハラスメント対策について

当社にてパワハラの事実が判明しました。当人たちとは話し合いを進め、解決に向けて動いています。今後、このような事例がないようガイドラインを作成しました。

各自必ずしっかりと読んで内容を確認してください。

人事部
花田カオリ

Subject: Anti-harassment measures

We have confirmed a case of harassment at our company. We are now holding talks with the people involved and are working towards a solution. To prevent such cases from happening in the future, we have created a manual with specific guidelines.

Please be sure to carefully read and confirm the information in this manual.

Kaori Hanada
HR Department

言い換えセンテンス

この事実に対して会社としてもフォローアップを行います。
The company will also follow up on this matter.

このようなことが起きないように各自の自覚が必要です。
Each of us needs to be aware of what we are doing to prevent this from happening.

ハラスメントに関する講座の開催が決定しました。
A course on harassment will be held.

ハラスメントに関するガイドラインを添付いたします。
Guidelines on harassment are attached.

就業規則を読み返してください。
Please read the work rules again.

弊社でのフォローアップのフローは以下の通りになります。
Our follow-up flow is as follows:

報告や相談などは複数人で行います。
Reports and consultations are conducted by multiple people.

個人情報はきちんと守ります。

We will ensure the protection of personal information.

以下にパワハラの例を挙げておきますので必ずご確認ください。

Here are some examples of power harassment. Please be sure to read this information carefully.

弊社で過去に相談のあったハラスメントの一覧をお送りいたします。

We will send you a summary of harassment reports that we have received in the past.

ガイドラインをよく読み、再発防止に努めてください。

Please read the guidelines carefully and try to prevent recurrence.

会社としては社員全員が気持ちよく働ける環境作りをしていきます。

As a company, we will create an environment in which all employees can work comfortably.

ハラスメントについて詳しく知りたい方は私宛てにご連絡をください。

If you would like to know more about harassment, please contact me.

他にもお悩みの方がいたら、ぜひ申し出てください。

If you have any concerns, please ask for help.

1人で問題を抱えずに必ず誰かに相談するようにしてください。

Instead of keeping your problems to yourself, always try to talk with someone.

困ったことがあれば、人事部の花田カオリ宛てにご相談ください。

If you have any questions, please contact Kaori Hanada in Human Resources.

ハラスメントを受けていると感じたら迷わずご相談ください。

If you feel that you are being harassed, please do not hesitate to contact us.

ハラスメントと思われる現場を見た方はご一報ください。

Please let us know if you see something that might be harassment.

ⓕ 社内イベントの告知

件名：忘年会のお知らせ

皆様

今年も残すところわずかとなりました。そこで忘年会を開催いたします。

日時：12 月 5 日　午後 6 時～ 9 時
場所：イタリアンテーブル

年末で忙しいとは思いますが、楽しい時間を過ごせたらと思います。

ご参加お待ちしております。

山本翔太

Subject: Year-end party notice

Hi everyone,

There are only a few days left this year, so we're planning a year-end party.

Date and time: December 5, 6:00-9:00 p.m.
Place: Italian Table

We know you are busy at the end of the year, but we hope everyone can join us for a good time.

We're looking forward to seeing you.

Shota Yamamoto

言い換えセンテンス

リモートで歓迎会をしたいと思います。
I would like to have a remote welcome party.

以下の通り防災訓練を実施いたします。
We will hold a disaster drill as follows.

田中さんの送別会 / 歓迎会を行います。
We are planning a farewell/welcome party for Tanaka-san.

出欠の連絡はメールで私宛てにお願いします。
Please send me an email letting me know if you can attend or not.

参加される場合は今週の金曜日までにご連絡ください。
Please let me know by this Friday if you will be attending.

リンダに花束を贈呈する予定ですので、5 時に営業部にお集まりください。
We will be presenting Linda with a bouquet of flowers, so please meet in the Sales Department at 5:00.

Zoom のリンクは会議の 1 時間前にお送りします。

The Zoom link will be sent an hour before the meeting.

都合がつく日時はありますか？

Is there a day and time that works for you?

大変お手数ですが、ご都合のつくお日にちを来週中にお知らせいただけると幸いです。

We would appreciate it if you could let us know when you're available by the end of next week.

遅れて参加される方は幹事の渡辺さんか広田さんに連絡してください。

If you're going to be late, please contact the organizers, Watanabe-san or Hirota-san.

時間内は出入り自由です。

You are free to come and go as you please.

時間は 2 時間程度を予定しています。

It will last about two hours.

強制参加ではありません。

Participation is not mandatory.

11 月末日までに部署ごとの出欠表を幹事まで提出して下さい。

Please submit the attendance sheet for each department to the secretary by the end of November.

今回、幹事は総務部の小林ツトムが務めますのでよろしくお願いします。

Tsutomu Kobayashi in the General Affairs Department will serve as the planner this time.

当日の急な連絡は以下の私の携帯番号までお願いします。

If you have any urgent questions on the day of the event, please call my cell phone number below.

可能な限りご参加いただきますようお願いいたします。

We encourage you to attend if at all possible.

お忙しいとは思いますが、業務のスケジュール調整をしてご参加ください。

I know you are busy, but please adjust your work schedule so you can join us.

⑨ 社内発表

件名：新規プロジェクト

皆様

弊社の新規プロジェクトが来年１月よりスタートすることになりました。

DEF 社と協力してアメリカで事業を展開します。新たな分野への大きな挑戦になりますが、会社の発展に向けた大きな一歩となるでしょう。

正式発表までは社外秘としてください。

ありがとうございます。
山本翔太

Subject: New project

Hello everyone,

I'd like to let you know that a new project will start from next January.

In cooperation with DEF, we will work on developing our business within the United States. This will be a big challenge for us in a new field, and it will be a big step in the development of the company.

Please keep this information confidential until the official announcement.

Thanks,
Shota Yamamoto

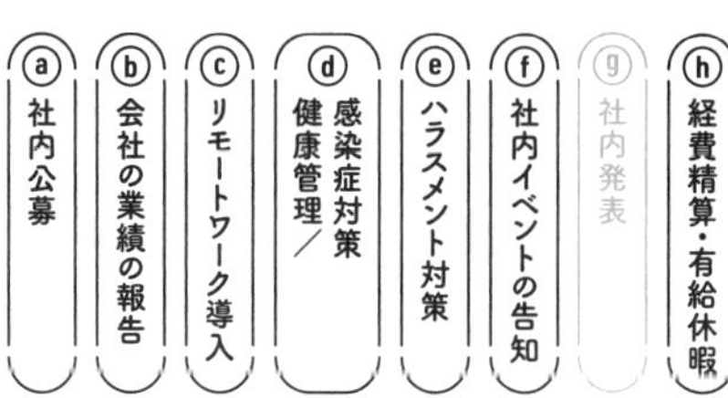

言い換えセンテンス

プロジェクトの内容は添付の通りです。
The details of the project are as attached.

海外進出することになりました。
We have decided to expand overseas.

新規プロジェクトが大成功を収めました。
The new project was a huge success.

目標額を大幅に上回りました。
We far exceeded the target amount.

弊社の新製品の売れ行きが好調です。
Sales of our new products are strong.

今年の夏季休暇は以下の通りになります。
This year's summer vacation is as follows.

創業以来の大ヒット商品となりました。
It has become our bestselling product since the company was founded.

皆様の協力なくしてはなしえませんでした。
We couldn't have done this without the support of everyone.

DEF 社との大型契約にこぎ着けました。
We got a big contract with DEF.

今年の勤続表彰の皆さんを発表いたします。
We are pleased to announce the service awards for this year.

先月の営業売上の優秀者は以下の通りです。
The following people had the best sales for last month:

表彰式はオンラインで行います。
The awards ceremony will be held online.

受賞者には賞状と記念品が贈られます。
Winners will receive a certificate and a commemorative gift.

受賞おめでとうございます。
Congratulations on receiving the prize!

この調子で売上を伸ばしていけたらと思います。
I hope we can continue to increase sales at this pace.

引き続き皆様のご協力をお願いします。

We ask for your continued cooperation.

これも皆様のたゆまぬ努力のおかげです。

We'd like to thank everyone for your tireless efforts.

ⓗ 経費精算・有給休暇

件名：有給休暇取得について

有給休暇についてのお知らせです。

労働基準法の改正により、年間 10 日以上有給休暇を付与される社員を、年間で少なくとも 5 日は取得するよう指導することが会社に義務づけられました。未取得者がいる場合は罰金が会社に科せられます。

有給休暇は労働者の心身の疲労回復、生産性の向上などにつながりますので積極的に取得してください。

ご質問があれば人事部の私宛にご連絡ください。

人事部
河合ケン

Subject: Taking paid leave

I have an announcement regarding paid leave.

Due to a revision to the Labor Standards Act, the company is now obligated to require employees who receive 10 or more days of paid leave per year to use at least five of those days. The company will be fined if you do not use your days.

Taking days off helps your body and mind recover and improves productivity, so please do not hesitate to use your days.

Please contact me in HR if you have any questions.

Ken Kawai
HR

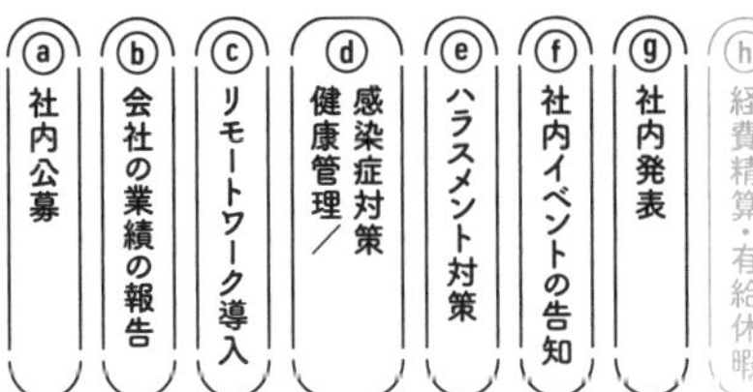

言い換えセンテンス

交通費精算についてのお知らせです。

I have an announcement regarding travel expenses.

取得日数が 5 日未満の社員には警告を出します。

A warning will be issued to employees who have not taken at least five days off.

年間の休暇取得スケジュールを提出してください。

Please submit your planned vacation days for the year.

半休 2 回を取得して 1 日とカウントしてもいいです。

If you take two half days off, you may count it as one day.

休みを取る際は業務に支障が出ないようにしてください。

If you take a day off, please make sure it does not interfere with your work.

管理者は休暇を取得しやすい環境を整えてください。

We ask managers to create an environment in which it is easy to take days off.

勤怠管理も部門責任者の業務の一つです。

One of the jobs of the department managers is to oversee attendance records.

社員による立替精算の締め切りは今月末です。

Employee expense reports are due at the end of this month.

交通経費は毎月精算してください。

Please calculate your travel expenses every month.

交通経費の精算には領収書が必要です。

Receipts are required to have your travel expenses reimbursed.

やむ得ない場合を除き、交通費は月ごとに精算してください。

Unless absolutely unavoidable, please calculate your travel expenses on a month-by-month basis.

交通費は月末にまとめて精算せずに発生後すぐに精算してください。

Please calculate your travel expenses immediately after traveling somewhere, not all at once at the end of the month.

月末は伝票が集中するため処理に時間がかかります。

We receive a lot of receipts at the end of the month, so it takes time to process all of them.

打ち合せ代は参加者の名前を全員記入してください。

Please write down the names of all the participants for meeting fee.

出張精算は出張から帰社後 5 営業日以内に提出してください。

Please submit your business trip expenses within five business days of returning.

交通費の精算では経路を明記してください。

Please write down the route you take to have your travel expenses reimbursed.

皆様のご協力をお願いいたします。

Thank you for your cooperation.

不明な点は経理部に直接お問い合わせください。

Please contact the Accounting Department directly if anything is unclear.

PART 3
ショートメッセージ集

① ウェブ会議

② 食事に誘う

③ スケジュール

④ 報告

⑤ 緊急

⑥ 気持ちを伝える

⑦ あいさつ

① ウェブ会議

音声を ON にしてください。

Please turn on your microphone.

雑音が入ってしまうので、音声はオフにしてください。

Please mute your microphone in case there is background noise.

音量をもっと上げてください。／下げてください。

Please turn your volume up. / Please turn your volume down.

音声が途切れています。

Your voice is cutting out.

音声にタイムラグがあります。

Your voice is lagging.

映像は見えていますが、音が聞こえません。

I can see you, but I can't hear you.

映像は切っていただいても大丈夫です。

You may turn off your video.

最初の挨拶のときだけ映像をオンにしてください。

Turn on your video only for the introductions at the start.

質問時以外は基本的にミュートにしてください。

Please mute your microphone except when asking questions.

画面は共有されていますか？

Is screen sharing working?

画面が共有されていません。

The screen share is not working.

画面をもっと大きくしてください。

Please make the screen bigger.

共有する画面が違っています。

You're sharing the wrong screen.

共有する画面はこれで合ってますか？

Am I sharing the right screen?

背景にご家族の方が映っていますよ。

We can see someone in your family in the background.

逆光で顔が見えていません。

I can't see your face because of the glare.

あなたの声しか聞こえません。

I can only hear your voice.

音声の調子が悪いみたいです。
We're breaking up a bit.

映像がオフになっています。
Your video is turned off.

ミュートになっていますよ。
You are muted.

音声が小さいようです。
Your sound is low.

鈴木さんの音声が途切れて聞こえます。
Mr. Suzuki's sound is cutting out.

画面が固まってしまっています。
The screen is frozen.

画面共有してください。
Please share your screen.

共有画面が見えづらいです。
It's hard to see your screen.

共有画面を大きくできますか？
Could you zoom in?

URL をチャットに送ってください。
Please send the URL to the chat.

質問はこちらのチャットに入れてください。

Please send questions to this chat.

スペルをチャットに送ってもらえますか?

Could you send the spelling to the chat?

会社名をチャットに入れてください。

Please send the company name to the chat.

ファイルをチャットにアップしてください。

Could you upload the file to the chat?

今日の会議の議事録をこのチャットにアップしておきます。

I'll send the report for today's meeting to this chat.

見せてはいけない書類を共有していますよ。

You're sharing some private documents.

お客様にその資料は見せてはいけないそうです。

Apparently you aren't allowed to show those materials to the customers.

背景に映ってはいけないものが映ってませんか?

Is something private showing in the background?

② 食事に誘う

リンダは最近忙しい?

Are you busy these days, Linda?

今日のランチ空いてますか?

Are you free to have lunch today?

明日のランチの予定は決まってる?

What are your plans for lunch tomorrow?

ちょっとランチに出ない?

Do you want to grab a bite for lunch?

今日のランチどうするの?

What are you doing for lunch today?

今夜ハルカと出かけるんだけど、一緒にどうですか?

I'll hang out with Haruka tonight. Do you feel like joining us?

今日は予定あり?

Do you have plans today?

明日は仕事の後何してるの?

What are you doing tomorrow after work?

私たちと一緒に飲みに行かない？

Would you like to have some drinks with us?

先週オープンしたバーに行くのはどう？

How about going to that bar which opened last week?

何を食べたい感じ？ 中華？ イタリアン？

What are you in the mood for? Chinese? Italian?

時間あるなら飲みに行かない？

If you're free, how about getting a drink?

ええ、行きましょう！

Yeah, let's go!

またにしておこうかな。

I'll take a rain check.

悪いけど、先約があるの。

Sorry, but I have another appointment.

金欠なんです。

I'm broke.

また今度。

Maybe next time.

ごめんね、ちょっと忙しくて。

I'm sorry, but I'm a little busy.

仕事が落ち着いたら飲みに行こうね！

Let's go get a drink when work has calmed down!

駅前の新しいカフェに行ってみたいな。

I want to try that new cafe by the station.

ケイトも誘っていい？

Do you mind if I ask Kate too?

仕事が終わったら後から合流するね！

We're going to meet up after work.

会社を出たら連絡してね！

Send me a message when you leave the office.

後から行くから先に２人で飲んでて。

I'll come a bit later, so you two start without me.

③ スケジュール

急用、病気、半休

急用ができたので、早退します。
Something urgent has come up, so I'll leave early.

体調が悪いので、本日は欠勤します。
I don't feel well, so I'll take today off.

朝病院に行ってから出社するので、半休をいただきます。
I'll go to the hospital this morning, so I'll take a half-day.

スケジュールの変更

スケジュールが変更となりました。
The schedule has changed.

会議は本日キャンセルとなりました。
Today's meeting has been cancelled.

会議の時間が 2 時間になりました。
The meeting duration has been changed to two hours.

場所が変更になりました。
The location has changed.

もう1件寄る 直帰する

これからもう1件クライアントの事務所へ向かいます。
I'm going to visit one more client.

今日はABCに寄ってからそのまま帰宅します。
I'll go to ABC and then go straight home from there.

明日のプレゼンの資料を作ったら帰宅します。
I'll go home after I've made the files for tomorrow's presentation.

今日は遅くまで残業になりそうです。
I think I'll have to work late tonight.

④ 報告

開始

作業を 9 時からスタートします。

Work will start from 9:00.

イベントが時間通りにスタートします。

The event will start on time.

会議が始まりました。

The meeting has started.

途中経過

途中経過を報告します。

I'll update you on the progress.

今のところ順調に進んでいます。

Things are progressing well.

少し遅れ気味です。

We're running a little behind.

完了・終了

イベントが無事に終了しました。

The event finished without any problems.

ファイルを確認したので、戻します。

I've checked the file, so I'll sending back.

結果

イベントは成功に終わりました。

The event finished successfully.

打ち合わせはうまくいきました。

The meeting went well.

打ち合わせですが、いまいちうまくいきませんでした。

The meeting didn't go well.

プレゼンが無事に終わりました。

- The presentation went off without a hitch.
- I've finished the presentation.

プレゼンはとてもうまくいきました。

The presentation went really well.

契約が取れました！

We got the contract!

⑤ 緊急

急かす

みなさん集まっているので、急いできてください。

Everyone is here, so please come quickly.

ファイルを至急メールで送ってください。

Please send the file by email immediately.

連絡をすぐにください。

Please contact me immediately.

呼び出す

事務所に至急戻ってください。

Please hurry back to the office.

来客の方がお待ちですので、会社に戻ってください。

A client is waiting for you, so please come back to the office.

リマインダー

10 時半から ABC 社との会議です。

The meeting with ABC is from 10:30.

本日 1 時が締め切りなので、お忘れなく。

Don't forget about the deadline at 1:00 today.

問題発生

お客様からクレームが来ています。
A customer has sent a complaint.

商品がまだ届いていないそうです。
The products haven't arrived yet.

担当者から、緊急の連絡が入っています。
There's an emergency call from the person in charge.

遅刻

今日 ABC 社で打ち合わせですが、遅れそうです。
I have a meeting at ABC today, but I may be late.

電車の事故で、会議に遅れそうです。
I'm going to be late for the meeting due to a train accident.

電車の復旧がいつになるかわかりません。
I don't know when the train will start again.

約束の時間に遅れてしまいそうです。
I'm not going to get there by the arranged time.

ABC 社のホワイトさんの連絡先を至急教えてください。
Please let me know the contact details of Mr. White at ABC as soon as possible.

⑥ 気持ちを伝える

感謝

ありがとう！

Thanks a lot!

手伝ってくれてありがとう。

Thanks for your help!

メールしてくれてありがとう。

Thanks for sending out the email.

いつもありがとう。

Thanks as always!

お詫び

会議に遅れてごめんね。

Sorry for being late for the meeting.

さっきは言いすぎてごめんなさい。

I'm sorry for overstepping the boundaries.

あなたを誤解してごめんなさい。

I'm sorry for misunderstanding you.

全部お任せしちゃってごめんね。

Sorry for dumping everything on you.

励まし

失敗は誰でもするからね。

Everyone makes mistakes.

気にしない方がいいよ！

Don't worry about it.

次また頑張ればいいよ。

You'll do better next time.

みんな怒ってないから大丈夫だよ。

No one's angry, so it's no problem.

おいしいものでも食べて忘れよう！

Let's have something delicious and forget about it.

プレゼンすごくよかったよ。

Your presentation was really good.

資料とてもよくできてるよ。

The materials were excellent.

仕事が本当に早くて正確だよね。

Your work is always fast and accurate.

WEB デザインにとっても詳しいんだね。

You really know a lot about web design.

教えてくれたお店すごくよかったよ。ありがとう!

The restaurant you told me about was great. Thanks!

そんなに落ち込まないで。

Don't let it get you down.

彼はいつも怒ってばかりだよね。

He always gets angry.

あなたが才能あるから注意するんだと思うよ。

I think he gets angry at you because you're talented.

チャンスはまた必ず来るよ。

You'll have another opportunity soon.

クヨクヨしても仕方ないよ。

Don't let it bother you.

私も同じような失敗したことあるよ。

I've made that mistake too.

誰でも最初は失敗するものだよ。

Everyone makes mistakes at first.

今日はおごるよ!

I'll treat you!

⑦ あいさつ

一般的なあいさつ

おはよう。
Good morning.

お疲れさまでした！
Thank you for your hard work!

また明日ね。／また月曜日ね。
See you tomorrow. / See you on Monday.

仕事のあと飲みに行かない？
How about a drink after work?

ランチに行かない？
Would you like to go out for lunch?

寒いから風邪ひかないようにね。
It's freezing, so don't catch a cold.

クリスマス、新年、祭日

よいクリスマスを！
Have a Merry Christmas!

週末に会おうね！
Let's meet up on the weekend!

忘年会／新年会やりましょうよ。

Let's have a year-end party / New Year's party.

よい連休を！

Have a nice holiday!

旅行、気をつけて行ってきてね。

Have a safe trip!

別れ（転職）

元気でね。

Take care.

別の会社でも元気でね。

Have fun at your new job!

連絡取り合おうね。

Let's keep in touch.

新しい職場からもメールちょうだいね。

Please email me from your new workplace.

アメリカからもメッセージ送ってね。

Send me a message from the US.

誕生日

誕生日おめでとう！

Happy birthday!

いい誕生日を過ごしてね！
Have a nice birthday!

パーティーしよう！
Let's party!

結婚

結婚おめでとう！
Congratulations on getting married!

今度旦那様を紹介してね。
I'm looking forward to meeting your husband.

結婚式は呼んでね。
Be sure to invite me to your wedding.

末長くお幸せにね。
I'm sure you're going to be happy together.

出産

出産おめでとう！
Congratulations on your new baby!

赤ちゃんの写真送ってね。
Please send me a picture of your baby.

手伝えることがあったら言ってね。
Please let me know if you need any help.

赤ちゃんの名前は決まった？

Have you chosen a name yet?

無理しないで過ごしてね。

Try to take it easy.

昇進

昇進おめでとう！

Congratulations on the promotion!

あなたならきっとやると思ってた。

I knew you would succeed.

やっと会社が認めてくれたね。

Your company has finally recognized your skills.

会社はあなたの頑張りをきちんと見てるよ。

It looks like the company has a lot of expectations for you.

あれだけ成果を出したんだから当然だよね。

You really worked hard, so I'm not surprised by this promotion.

私も昇進できるようにがんばるね！

I'll do my best to get promoted too!

お見舞い

風邪の具合はどうですか？

How is your cold?

きっと疲れてるんだね。
You must be tired.

無理しちゃだめだよ。
Try to take it easy.

周りにきちんと手伝ってもらってね。
Make sure you ask your coworkers for help.

よくなるまでゆっくり休んでね。
Take it easy until you get better.

入院先の病院を教えてもらえる?
Could you tell me where you're hospitalized?

お見舞いに行ってもいい?
Is it okay if I visit you?

お見舞いに行けなくてごめんね。
I'm sorry I couldn't go see you in the hospital.

早く良くなって!
Get well soon!

Feel better soon! でも OK

お悔やみ

お父さまのこと聞きました。
I heard the sad news about your father.

なんと言えばよいのか分かりません。
I don't know what to say.

あなたの気持ちを思うと、胸が痛みます。
My heart hurts when I think of how you must feel.

こんな辛い時はどうか無理しないでね。
Please try to take it easy during this difficult time.

話したいときはいつでも連絡ください。
Please feel free to call me if you ever need to talk to someone.

手伝えることがあったら遠慮しないでね。
If I can do anything to help, don't hesitate to ask.

待ち合わせ

どこにいる?
Where are you?

ごめん! 遅れそうです!
Sorry! I'm going to be late!

先にお店に入ってて。
Go inside without me.

あと 5 分で着きそうです。
I'll get there in five minutes.

道に迷ってます。
I'm lost.

仲間と飲み会

今夜飲み会なのでお忘れなく！
Don't forget the party tonight!

今夜 7 時からオンライン飲み会しよう！
Let's have an online drinking party from 7:00 tonight!

お店にもう着いてます！
I'm already at the restaurant.

あなたとマイクが来れば全員そろいます。
We're just waiting on you and Mike!

先に始めてます！
We're starting without you!

遅くなってもいいから、待ってるよ！
Don't worry if you come late, we'll be here!

もう盛り上がってるよ～！
Everyone's having a good time!

先に始めてるから、慌てないでいいからね。
We've already started, so no need to rush.

あ

か

さ

た

	response	114 134 143 144 155 340 343 379
報告(報告書、報告する)	report	042 268 322 323 324 325 327 328 331 332 351 352 373 412 413 414 415 425 426 438 445
	update	027 038 451

み

見積もり	estimate	031 119 144 145 146 147 148 149 152 153 156 160 161 229
	quotation	145 146 147 149 150 153 156 157 159
	quote	145 146 152 158 162
面会(約束)	appointment	061 174 447
申し出(提案)	offer	056 058 161 162 194 196 197 198 199 224
問題(課題、トラブル)	problem	005 035 038 039 119 127 153 166 170 172 176 181 183 200 219 258 268 277 279 280 283 284 289 324 348 362 363 368 378 384 389 404 413 427 451 456
	issue	057 133 200 212 213 256 275 276 279 282 283 287 389 414
	trouble	062 133 239 261 266 282 377 392

や

休みを取る	take something off	436 437 449

ら

理解(理解する)	understand	035 042 099 163 239 240 241 242 247 311 323 389 423
	make sense	207
リンク	link	088 089 091 135 138 351 402 404 430

デイビッド・セイン（David Thayne）

（株）AtoZ English 代表。米国生まれ。証券会社勤務後に来日。日本での 30 年にわたる英語指導の実績を生かし、英語学習書、教材、Web コンテンツの制作を手掛ける。累計 400 万部を超える著書を刊行、多くがベストセラーとなっている。オフィシャルサイト：https://www.smartenglish.co.jp/

英文ビジネス E メール大全

2022 年 4 月 20 日　初版発行

著　者　デイビッド・セイン　
発行者　伊藤秀樹
発行所　株式会社 ジャパンタイムズ出版
〒 102-0082　東京都千代田区一番町 2-2　一番町第二 TG ビル 2F
電話 050-3646-9500 [出版営業部]
ウェブサイト https://jtpublishing.co.jp/
印刷所　株式会社光邦

Printed in Japan　ISBN 978-4-7890-1812-8

本書のご感想をお寄せください。
https://jtpublishing.co.jp/contact/comment/